To the 30 geniuses
who attended my 40th birthday party...
and Ken

Copyright © 2016 Aaron Clarey

All rights reserved. No part of this publication may be reproduced, distributed, or transmitted in any form or by any means, including photocopying, recording, or other electronic or mechanical methods, without the prior written permission of the publisher, except in the case of brief quotations embodied in critical reviews and certain other noncommercial uses permitted by copyright law. For permission requests, contact Aaron Clarey

TABLE OF CONTENTS

Foreword	1
Introduction	5
The Needs of Many	17
Idiocracy	29
Education	50
Career	82
Socializing, Dating, & Marriage	117
Psychology	156
Limiting Greatness	176
Solutions	199

FOREWORD
BY MATT BALDONI

It's not often that you go from fan to friend in the arts world. As a musician, I've had the opportunity to meet a few of my musician heroes personally, but never become friends with them. I do have talented friends and colleagues in my business and in other fields of art, and most of them inspire me at least a little bit. None as much as Aaron does.

I was introduced to his material by simple recommendation and became a fan very quickly. I watched videos, purchased books, downloaded podcasts, and added his material as part of my life's routine until the material became a powerful influence that changed my life. Upon realizing this, I reached out to thank him. A few years later, we are close and personal friends, and I remain one of his biggest fans. Becoming friends with someone whom you're this big of a fan of is an honor and can change your life.

When Cappy Cap announced to me that he was writing another book, and the subject was High IQ, we discussed it and shared ideas about it. As usual with his books, I became interested and excited to eventually buy it and read it as a fan. When he asked me if I'd like to contribute to this work, a second life-changing honor occurred, and I happily accepted. For me, this was like a musical hero asking me to play on his record or sit in with him on a gig. Now that I have read the work and understand its message, I can safely say that it's my favorite work of Aaron's so far, and it may be his most powerful book yet.

Those of us who are fans of his will know his work's message(s) well. He speaks to young people, particularly men, about how to live an optimized life in most every way. Education, finance, dating, friendships, health, hobbies, romantic relationships, and many more subjects are all covered in his books, podcasts, videos, and consultations. Those of us who know him will know without a doubt that he is an expert enough to demand damn good money for his advice and thoughts.

Perhaps for some of you, this is your first time reading one of Aaron Clarey's books. If that's the case, I have some advice for you. Prepare to be reaffirmed in many opinions you may already have, but felt you needed to keep quiet due to societal pressures/conditions, professional aspirations, or friends and loved ones. One thing all of us who are fans have in common is that we love that there's someone who says what we've all been thinking.

I'll also advise that you keep going deeper into Aaron's prolific catalog after reading this book. "Bachelor Pad Economics" is the mens' encyclopedia for life, "Worthless" has saved young people thousands of dollars and years of shame, "Behind The Housing Crash" predicted the near-collapse of the U.S. Economy and tells you why, and "Captain Capitalism: Top Shelf" and "Reserved" are the quintessential collections from his blog writings, allowing you to not only learn from his expertise but witness his evolution and growth as a writer, which is remarkable. I advise all those new to Captain Capitalism to dig deep and read EVERYTHING. TWICE.

One night recently on a gig, I had the opportunity to spend time with someone I can easily equate to Aaron Clarey. This gentleman is also a staunch libertarian, an intelligent and high-level thinker with a likely-high IQ, an entertainment hero of mine, and a personal friend. The man I am speaking of is magician Penn Jillette, my personal hero in Las Vegas entertainment. He and I spoke of Aaron Clarey that night, and he was familiar. This brought a huge smile to my face, and I walked out onto a stage that night to receive an award for Entertainer of The Year here in Las Vegas.

As Penn looked on smiling from side-of-stage, I thought of us just speaking of Aaron. As I accepted the award and took a bow amidst the applause, I thought to myself, *"There's no way you'd be getting this tonight without Aaron."* That is no lie. The guy'll change your life.

I also can't help but remember the time that Aaron and I stood at the near-top of an 11,000 foot peak in rural Nevada, talking to each other about the journey up that far, and admiring the view with smiles on our faces. The mountain and our journey to the top is a metaphor for life. Aaron has written in nearly all of his works that "the most important part of life is other human beings". They are the ones that help you get to the top of that mountain where you can enjoy the view and survey your domain from a new place in life. I am one of the lucky guys to call Aaron a friend who's helped me get there, and after you read this book, you will feel the same.

Matt Baldoni
www.mattbaldoni.com
Las Vegas, January 2016

INTRODUCTION

Highly Successful, Miserable Freaks

Mike was 43 and although his real estate business took a terrible turn during the housing crash, he was one of the few who survived it. He made wise decisions, cut the budget as necessary, and with some hard work and clever investments he recovered nicely. He had his dream cabin up north as well as a schwank James Bond early 60's style house in the city all in his name. A nice gun collection to pursue his passion of hunting with. And free time. Loads of free time as he would read books, watch Black Adder, and pursue his various entrepreneurial ideas plastered on the white board in his office.

He was his own man. He answered to no one. He was living the dream.

Jeff was also very successful. After selling his stake in a small business at 46, he started his own special materials transport company. He moved to Las Vegas to avoid the Minnesota winters and, again, with some wise decisions and hard work was clearing nearly half a million a year in profit. With this profit came a lifestyle of luxury and free time he never experienced before, but one he certainly capitalized on, affording himself a fine cigar hobby, frequent travel, a Harley, not to mention courtships with one or two (perhaps three or four...certainly no more than five or six) girls half his age.

He too was his own man. Answered to no one. And was living the dream.

And then there was Tony. Tony was a major in the US Army tortured about whether to stay his 20 years and collect a pension. Not that he needed the money - he was a minimalist and took whatever money he didn't spend and invested it in rental property. But his simplistic and frugal lifestyle allowed him a freedom few other 35 year olds had. He could sample the finest scotches at the finest bars in Miami as his studio apartment was in an enviable neighborhood. He also, perhaps, sampled some of the finest ladies the town had to offer as he was devastatingly charming, incredibly witty, but also a master at meting it out at opportune moments.

He too, like Mike and Jeff, was his own man. Answered to no one. And was living the dream.

So why were they all miserable?

Mike, for all of his success and free time, seemed hell-bent to stay in his basement, wishing to do nothing more than watch BBC comedies. I could rarely get him to go out, but when I did he was nowhere near as animated as when I knew him in his youth. He was in his pajamas usually by 7PM, asking me if I wanted milk or tea. And even though the sun had yet to set, when I inquired if he wanted to go out for dinner, coffee, or a run it was always too close to his bedtime to contemplate such "excitement."

Jeff, with all the money (and girls) a man could want, was constantly inquiring if I could fly down and visit him in Vegas. I explained I'd love to, but time and financial constraints prevented me from doing so. *"No problem"* he said, *"you can stay in my other apartment the entire time free of charge! And you can use my other car for free too!"* Combine this with his frequent calls to chat, it became very apparent he could not find a social network in Vegas and it was actually easier for him to fly his friends down there.

And Tony? Yeah...Tony.

Hammered. All the time. Only allowing sobriety to interrupt him during work. Something was haunting him. Something so fierce and dark he could have two girls on his arms, both likely to go home with him, and would trade it in for another drink and the opportunity to talk philosophy with you. He had life by the tail and couldn't care less if he let it go.

The simple answer to the mystery of my highly successful, yet miserable friends would have been one of coincidence or chance. So what? Three friends of mine are incredibly successful, but miserable? It happens, besides nobody's life is perfect. And that would have been a satisfactory answer had my mind not made another observation. For it wasn't just Mike, Jeff, and Tony who shared the three unique traits of being

highly interesting
successful, yet
miserable

but nearly all of my friends.

John. Successful jazz singer. Voice you'd kill for. Traveled the world. Constant state of depression.

Greg. Retired millionaire. Drives around North America with his dog in a van. Has no place to call home.

Alyssa. Incredibly talented and successful musician. Can't find any equals, spends most nights alone and down because she can't pursue her art as she's so reliably employed.

Mark. Lives on a beach and a pension. Hotter than hell wife. So crippled by the fate of the country he can barely leave the house.

Phil. IT genius millionaire. Charges $300 an hour. Does nothing but drink coffee and teach himself languages at home. Occasionally shows up at Perkins.

Amy. Also an IT genius. Bills the same hourly rate as Phil. Can't find a guy to stimulate her. Stays at home with her dog.

Steve. High level administrator at a government agency, plus ballroom dancer. Miserable with his wife and life.

Travis. Perpetually unemployed. Alcoholic. Best philosopher I know.

Eric. House bought and paid for. Wife, two kids. In a constant state of anger due to the state of the country.

Jessica. Rare female oil field worker. Makes great money. Company grooming her for management because of affirmative action/political/marketing. She just wants a family that she's never going to have.

Ryan. Senior pilot at a large airline. Business on the side. Nice house. No debt. Can't find a girl to save his life.

I could go on, but as I thought about it nearly every friend I had, as well as myself, was a highly successful, interesting, statistical freak leading great lives, with great friends, who ironically were on some level, miserable, even dysfunctional. And upon having that epiphany it soon dawned on me what the common variable might be.

"Mike! What's your IQ?" I asked.

"What do you mean, what's my IQ?" he asked.

I said, *"You're IQ! What is it!?"*

"127. Why?"

I called Jeff.

"Jeff! What's your IQ?"

"My IQ???"

"Yeah, your IQ? Ever have it tested?"

"Yeah, when I was a kid, I think it was 138 or something."

"Tony?"

"157."

"John?"

"132"

Greg, 144.
Alyssa, 158.
Mark, 127.
Phil, 133.
Amy, 130.
Steve, 129.
Travis, 137
Eric, 140.
Jessica, 152
Ryan, 138
Me, 141.

I had figured it out. I had the common variable.

Yes, we were all very successful. And yes, we were all "eccentric" in one way or another. But while an argument can be made that this was selection bias, a mere preference to hang out with like-minded people, it was the freakishly high IQ's that explained the misery component of my cabal of friends. For in taking inventory of my friends, the nature of their problems, and the sources of their misery, as well as combining it with my own experiences, observations, research, and theories, this correlation made it increasingly clear that:

1. Our problems were not unique, but shared and common among people with high IQ's (depression, alcoholism, ennui, indifference, loneliness, boredom, etc.), and
2. It was being caused by abnormally high intelligences that unintentionally ostracized us from the rest of society.

Alas, if having a high IQ was wreaking similar problems on others across the world, not only did we know the cause, we also held the solution. And so instead of suffering in silence, thinking there was something specifically and uniquely wrong with us, it was imperative we brought this to the attention of those who are abnormally intelligent in the world. For if we're right, millions of people are needlessly suffering the same, enduring lesser lives than they should. Worse, they likely have no idea why and are therefore unable to solve their problems. But it doesn't have to be this way, and this essay intends to prove that. We can lift the curse of the high IQ.

The Truth

The truth is, just like any other trait or characteristic, having an abnormally high intelligence has both pros and cons. However, since being intelligent is largely viewed as a positive by society, we often erroneously attribute any problems caused by it to something else because,

"You're intelligent. How can anything bad possibly come from that?"

This misdiagnosis (like all misdiagnoses) is bound to fail since it misidentifies the true source of our problems, treating the "wrong source." It also makes the problem worse in that you never solve it resulting in hopelessness, futility, angst, despair, not to mention the insanity of being unable to know what's wrong with you.

The key, however, is to acknowledge there are problems with having a high IQ and to identify them. And while this essay will delve into much greater detail about these problems, they all predominantly hail from one primary source - statistics and economies to scale.

Statistically speaking, we're freaks. This is neither good nor bad, just merely different. However, in being a statistical oddity there comes an inherent lack of efficiency in that we cannot capitalize or benefit from the economies to scale that exist to serve the vast majority of the population which happens to be less intelligent than us.

For example if you're average and wish to make friends and socialize you have a plethora of options available to you. You can go to a nightclub, you can go to the bars, you can "watch the game," or join a fantasy football league. No doubt for some of you this sounds appetizing, but for the majority of high IQ people these are painful experiences as they lack the mental stimulation we need and thus, to us, are pointless.

Another example, night owls. People with high IQ's tend not to be able to sleep well and do their best work at night. Unfortunately, the rest of the world doesn't work that way and is on the traditional 9-5 schedule. This means you cannot avail yourself of the "economies to scale" and infrastructure that exists to serve the majority of the population during the day time. Restaurants are closed at 3AM so you are relegated to unhealthy gas station food (if they're open). Home Depot is also closed so if you're working on your latest great invention and need a tool, too bad for you. But while these minor inconveniences may seem petty and not really problems, worse is the lack of human interaction. Nobody is up at 3AM and so you are by yourself, in the dark, and in the quiet. Over time this WILL lead to psychological troubles, all because your intelligence prevents you from holding a normal sleep schedule.

We could go on, but the the larger point is there ARE problems that stem from having a high IQ. Many of which are minor. Many of which are serious. And like any other medical or psychological condition we need to be able to identify its root cause if we are ever to hope to solve it. But since society is largely geared around serving the "normal majority" and having a high IQ is viewed as a blessing, not a curse, the problems caused by having a high IQ are ignored by society, even ourselves, forcing an unnecessary (and often misunderstood) misery into our lives.

The Solution

The purpose of this book is to identify, explain, and provide solutions to the problems that are inherent in having a high IQ. This ranges from addressing the obvious psychological and sociological problems smart people have, to the fact that many smart people believe themselves to be stupid simply because they fall asleep in class. But regardless of the problem, the overall aim is to help the average high IQ person understand what it means to have a high IQ, realize the disadvantages that come with it, be able to accurately diagnose any problems deriving from it, and therefore develop reality-based solutions that will be effective in solving them.

This isn't a promise that all the problems abnormally intelligent people suffer will go away. Matter of fact, many of these problems have no solution as they're just inherent to the nature of statistics and your only option is to suck it up and endure it. But at minimum we can provide an explanation as to why you're feeling down, why you drink, why you can't find friends, why you can't hold a job, etc. It may not result in happiness, sobriety, or an active social life, but it will at least provide an explanation and the precious sanity that comes with it.

CHAPTER 1
THE NEEDS OF THE MANY

Cold, Hard Math

As alluded to in the introduction, problems stemming from being abnormally intelligent are largely seeded in math. Specifically, there are so few people with high IQ's that by statistical necessity they are invariably going to suffer in one capacity or another. This does not mean there is anything inherently wrong in having a high (or low) IQ, but at times being so intelligent will be inefficient, or at least inconvenient when it comes to interacting with the rest of society.

To understand this, however, one needs to know just how intelligent they are compared to the rest of society. This will allow them to see just what a statistical outlier they are and how few equally-intelligent people exist in the world. But what is very interesting about abnormally intelligent people is they rarely look at their intelligence in this manner. Matter of fact, most high IQ people aren't even aware they're intelligent because they've never had their IQ tested, or worse, were never led to believe they were smart in the first place. It's not until you test your intelligence and measure it up against the rest of society do you realize the statistical consequences and hurdles you will face in being abnormally intelligent.

To do this we use the classical "bell distribution" model used in statistics. Depending on your age you may or may not be familiar with this tool, but it requires nothing more than 3rd grade math and is merely a way to calculate where you rank as a percentage of the population in terms of intelligence. To calculate your percent ranking or "percentile" you need a few variables:

1. Your IQ (which you can get by taking a professionally administered test or by taking any one number of IQ tests online which will give you a less accurate, though ball park number)
2. The average or "mean" score of the population's IQ
3. The "standard deviation" of the population's IQ, and
4. A "Z-Score" table

Thankfully, we have most of these variables as IQ tests and scores have been standardized over the years and we have been able to historically measure them.

The average IQ score is benchmarked to 100 by default.

The standard deviation for IQ has historically been around 15.

And Z-Score tables can be found on the internet (one conveniently linked here)

http://www.utdallas.edu/dept/abp/zscoretable.pdf

With these four variables (your IQ being the fourth) the math to calculate your percentile ranking is pretty straight forward.

1. Take your IQ and subtract 100 from it (ensure to keep track if it is positive or negative)
2. Take that number and divide it by 15.
3. That number is your Z-Score
4. Look up your Z-Score on the Z-Score table. The corresponding number is your percentile rank and is the percent of the population that is BELOW you in terms of intelligence.

For example, let's use an IQ test score of 125.

1. 125-100 = 25
2. 25 divided by 15 is 1.67
3. 1.67 is my Z-Score so I look that up on the Z-Score table
4. Showing that 95.25% of the population has an IQ less than 125 or translated another way, "you are in the top 4.75% of the population in terms of intelligence."

z	0.00	0.01	0.02	0.03	0.04	0.05	0.06	0.07	0.08	0.09
0.0	0.5000	0.5040	0.5080	0.5120	0.5160	0.5199	0.5239	0.5279	0.5319	0.5359
0.1	0.5398	0.5438	0.5478	0.5517	0.5557	0.5596	0.5636	0.5675	0.5714	0.5753
0.2	0.5793	0.5832	0.5871	0.5910	0.5948	0.5987	0.6026	0.6064	0.6103	0.6141
0.3	0.6179	0.6217	0.6255	0.6293	0.6331	0.6368	0.6406	0.6443	0.6480	0.6517
0.4	0.6554	0.6591	0.6628	0.6664	0.6700	0.6736	0.6772	0.6808	0.6844	0.6879
0.5	0.6915	0.6950	0.6985	0.7019	0.7054	0.7088	0.7123	0.7157	0.7190	0.7224
0.6	0.7257	0.7291	0.7324	0.7357	0.7389	0.7422	0.7454	0.7486	0.7517	0.7549
0.7	0.7580	0.7611	0.7642	0.7673	0.7704	0.7734	0.7764	0.7794	0.7823	0.7852
0.8	0.7881	0.7910	0.7939	0.7967	0.7995	0.8023	0.8051	0.8078	0.8106	0.8133
0.9	0.8159	0.8186	0.8212	0.8238	0.8264	0.8289	0.8315	0.8340	0.8365	0.8389
1.0	0.8413	0.8438	0.8461	0.8485	0.8508	0.8531	0.8554	0.8577	0.8599	0.8621
1.1	0.8643	0.8665	0.8686	0.8708	0.8729	0.8749	0.8770	0.8790	0.8810	0.8830
1.2	0.8849	0.8869	0.8888	0.8907	0.8925	0.8944	0.8962	0.8980	0.8997	0.9015
1.3	0.9032	0.9049	0.9066	0.9082	0.9099	0.9115	0.9131	0.9147	0.9162	0.9177
1.4	0.9192	0.9207	0.9222	0.9236	0.9251	0.9265	0.9279	0.9292	0.9306	0.9319
1.5	0.9332	0.9345	0.9357	0.9370	0.9382	0.9394	0.9406	0.9418	0.9429	0.9441
1.6	0.9452	0.9463	0.9474	0.9484	0.9495	0.9505	0.9515	0.9525	0.9535	0.9545
1.7	0.9554	0.9564	0.9573	0.9582	0.9591	0.9599	0.9608	0.9616	0.9625	0.9633

While this method does in fact give you a good estimate as to where you rank in society in terms of intelligence, the problem in using Z-Score tables is that they're a bit complicated and fail to visually convey just what a statistical outlier you are. To do this it helps graph your intelligence on a bell distribution chart since IQ (as are many things in life) is not linear. In other words the majority (68%) of the population falls within one standard deviation of the average score, and the vast majority of the population (95%) falls within two standard deviations of the average score.

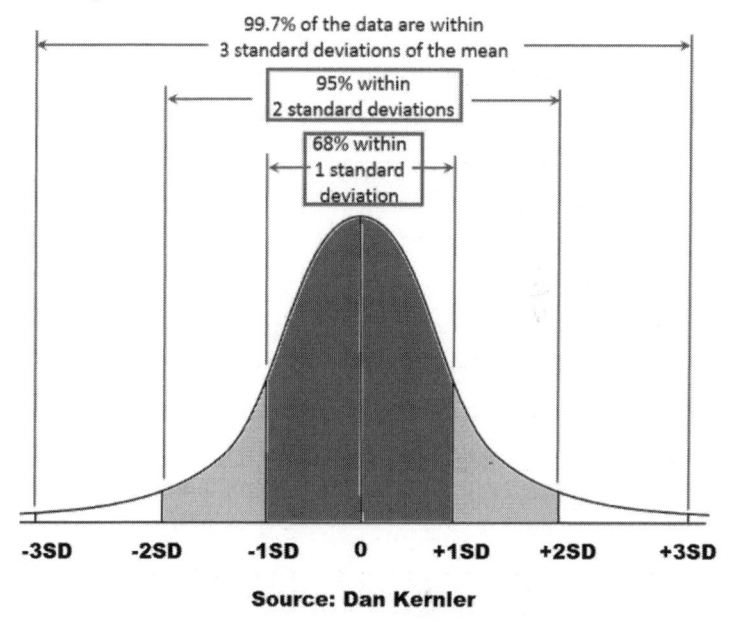

Source: Dan Kernler

Therefore, the percent of the population decreases exponentially faster the smarter and smarter you get, resulting in increasingly fewer people. Thus, once you start scoring in the 130+ range of IQ you are already in the top 2% of society. High enough to be considered an official genius by MENSA, but also most certainly a statistical freak.

Of course the issue is not whether you meet the 2% requirement MENSA has to officially be considered a genius. You can "merely" have an IQ of 120 and still suffer the consequences of having a high IQ. The larger point is to realize that as you go to (either) extremes of the bell distribution curve the population rapidly declines. And while there still may be enough of a population at an IQ of 115 where you can function relatively normally, you become increasingly statistically ostracized the further down the right of the bell curve you go.

Of course, all of this is moot if you don't first realize where you land in society in terms of intelligence. You, once again, will likely chalk your problems up to something that is NOT abnormal intelligence, misdiagnosing your problems, never being able to solve them. But if you can take the first step in finding out just what a statistical outlier you are, *especially visually*, it really puts the underlying problem of having a high IQ in perspective.

(To assist in being able to graphically visualize this there are many online bell distribution calculators. However, I prefer this one

http://mathcracker.com/normal_probability.php

The "population mean" is 100.
The "Population St. Dev." is 15
Select "Right Tailed" and then plug your IQ into that box.

After you hit submit it should generate a bell distribution chart below showing you your rank and percentile).

"This World is Not Meant for You"

Once you know your percentile rank and can see just how rare it is for someone to have your intelligence, you're going to quickly realize you are "special." And while "special" may have a positive connotation to it today, the world, sadly, was not built for special people.

Take for example physically handicapped people. They account for roughly the same percentage of the population that abnormally intelligent people do, but face daily hurdles most of us don't consider because we are not handicapped. Stairs, curbs, being unable to drive, things we take for granted simply on account we are not physically disabled. But it is not so much their physical disability that is the hurdle as much as it is this world was not designed with them in mind.

This world was designed for normal people. This world was designed for the majority.

Of course, this may sound unfair at first, but it's not because by mathematical necessity society *has to be* engineered around the majority. It cannot be designed for the minority on account that world would simply be too inefficient to work.

You can't have the highway system designed for the minority of the population, you need it to serve the cities and dense population centers.

You can't have an electric grid that first serves North Dakotan backwaters and then New York City.

And laws can't be written with specific groups or minorities in mind, it must be written with the majority in mind.

This doesn't meant we don't make accommodations for those who are disabled or different, but it is to point out that the social, political, economic, romantic, educational, commercial and psychological infrastructure of this society, its entire make up and composition on all levels, is built and designed for people with IQ's of around 100.

This guarantees you are going to have at least some problems when it comes to operating and living within this society. It can be as petty as the aforementioned problem of not being able to shop at Home Depot at 3AM because society typically operates on a 9-5 schedule. It could be the severe and real psychological problems that come from insomnia including depression, an impaired social life, poorer health, even suicide. But no matter the variety or severity of the problems it is the omnipresence of these problems that is the real challenge. In nearly every aspect of life your IQ is guaranteed to present at least some kind of problem.

That idiot in front of you at the gas station buying his cigarettes and lottery tickets with a check is not only delaying your day, but also likely driving up your blood pressure and taxes.

Your boss lacking the intelligence to understand Microsoft Excel views your expertise in Excel NOT as a way to save the company millions, but a threat that undermines his authority.

Your congressman wants to get re-elected, so instead of balancing a budget, runs a deficit buying him votes from the ignorant masses...but undermining your economic future as well.

And good luck finding a girl or a guy to date whose interests go beyond "The Kardashians" or "The New England Patriots," because their brains are not capable of enjoying any entertainment more intelligent than reality TV and "sportsball."

In nearly every capacity, aspect, and function in life you can expect hurdles to be put in front of you.

But it gets worse.

For while we can focus on careers, education, dating, entertainment, etc., having a high IQ undermines the most fundamental and important thing in our lives – society. Specifically, other people.

Whether we like it or not, we will derive 100% of our value and happiness from other people. You can have the latest PS4 video game with a 60 inch screen TV, a Ferrari, and a small island in your name, but it does not change the fact that without family, friends, loved ones and a social life all the material items in the world mean nothing. Additionally, we also need to function in society *outside of our circle of loved ones*, not only because we need jobs and have to interact with people on the street, but for the simple truism that there is no other society to function in. It's the only one available to us. This in an "eagle surrounded by turkeys" sense limits our success and happiness in life in that we need to rely, interact with, and depend on other people less intelligent than us.

Alas, every important aspect of your life is going to be, at some level, limited because the people you need to work with are also limited. This is your family. Your church. Your social club. Your neighbors. Your boss. Your spouse. Your friends. Your leaders. Your everything. Of course, this doesn't mean it's completely hopeless or that you're completely powerless to control who and who you don't let into your life. Obviously, you will choose friends as smart as you. Marry somebody at your intelligence level. Preferably work for a boss that is intelligent as well. But since there are so few abnormally intelligent people out there it is (frankly) unlikely your spouse, boss, co-workers, friends, colleagues, teachers, and neighbors are all going to be geniuses. And certainly not the everyday people you will need to interact with to go about your day to day business.

Suck it Up, Buttercup

But for all the problems associated with having a high IQ they are not as bad as being mentally impaired, physically handicapped, terminally ill, or any one of a

number of other more serious problems.
Additionally, having a high IQ has statistically proven to be a net asset with better financial success, physical health, life expectancy, etc. So, again, even though there are problems with having a high IQ it is important to put this into perspective.

But to put things into even further perspective, even the ultimate perspective, it simply doesn't matter that "this world was not meant for us" simply because it's the only one we got. It's the one we were born into. It was the hand we were dealt.

We need to adapt because there simply is no other choice. The world is not going to "adapt to us" with the majority magically increasing their IQ's through rigorous studies and genetic treatments. And if we focus on how "unfair" things might be or mire in our problems, we will simply never solve them ensuring we wasted our one finite, short, and precious life on this planet. So in short it is we who need to adapt. It is we who need to know where we fit in this world. And it is we who have to take an emotionless, somber assessment of the world around us, acknowledge it and work within it to solve whatever problems ail us from having a high IQ.

CHAPTER 2
IDIOCRACY

How Many Beers are in a Case?

Understanding where we sit statistically in the context of societal intelligence we can move onto more specific problems abnormally intelligent people will face. Specifically, the mental costs associated with living in an Idiocracy.

It was my senior year in high school and it was mandated we attend a rally where the guest speaker was our local congressional representative. Based on people's faces it was obvious I was not the only one who didn't want to attend. So when our congressman started asking the audience questions…only to receive no or begrudged answers…I decided we'd all get out of there a lot sooner if I were to answer one of his questions to accelerate his speech.

He asked the audience, *"How many members of congress are there?"*

Noticing nobody was going to answer I said, *"535."*

Thinking I cumulatively saved the entire student body two hours of their lives, a sophomore behind me tapped me on my shoulder and said, *"Hey, Einstein, how many beers are in a case?"*

Not knowing, nor really caring I said, *"I don't know, 12?"*

In a very Beavis and Butthead manner he snorted, *"Heh heh, it's 16! Shows you how much you know!"*

I could only think to myself, *"Yeah kid, it actually does."*

The truth is this young boy was retarded. And I don't mean that as an insult. I mean that because it's true. He was a mental retard. Not only did he think knowing how many beers are in a case was superior to knowing how many people are in our national legislature, he also had a ton of behavioral problems, suspensions, and...oh...yeah...thought it a good idea to tattoo a spider web around his eye. All of this before he could even get his driver's permit.

But the real reason he was a mental retard had nothing to do with

his underage drinking,

his idiocy in thinking it was "cool" to display his knowledge of beer trivia,
or his fine choice in ink.

No, the reason he was retarded is because it was in comparison to me.

The truth was this kid in all likelihood had a normal IQ of around 95. Not officially or clinically retarded, but no genius either. Just a normal, typical piece of Wisconsin trailer trash. But as far as what I experienced, what my brain personally interpreted and endured in relation to this kid was one of dealing with a severely retarded individual. For when you compare his normal IQ of 95 to my IQ of 138 the *relative experience* I endured was that of a normal person dealing with a severely mentally retarded individual.

This is a phenomenon most high IQ people don't realize. Since society is "normal" and by definition focuses around "average," so too is our language and standards. Therefore when we think "mentally retarded" we automatically think of someone who is *clinically* retarded (typically considered somebody with an IQ below 80). However, this is an *absolute* measure and not a *relative* one.

The idiot at my high school had an IQ about 43 points lower than me. ***Nearly a full THREE standard deviations lower.*** That would be like a normal person with an IQ of 100 interacting with a person with an IQ of 57. An IQ that only .2% (not 2%, ***.2%***) of the population has and is definitely considered mentally retarded. For a normal person it would be like dealing with somebody barely able to take care of themselves. However, since this idiot was "normal" by society's standards (capable of walking, talking, perhaps employment, and functioning normally) we focus on absolute intelligence instead of relative intelligence.

Still, this does not solve the problem that for those with incredibly high IQ's just dealing with your average person can be a painful experience as it is very much like dealing with a retard. This is not to belittle or besmirch those who have normal intelligence, let alone those with low intelligence, but it is to highlight that significant enough differences in IQ can result in an inordinate amount of frustration, angst, anger, and ultimately hopelessness as abnormally intelligent people try to interact with the rest of society.

Culture and Entertainment

At first you may find this claim (that normal people are "relatively retarded" to intelligent ones) to be a bit arrogant and condescending. But this book was not written for normal people, besides it just so happens to be true. High IQ individuals suffer an immeasurable amount of pain and agony due to IQ gaps. And this can be easily proven by looking at what passes for "culture and entertainment" in today's America.

The fact that "Keeping Up with the Kardashians," "The View," "Dr. Oz," and whatever slop they're serving up for prime time sitcoms today is the most consumed media out there is a testament to just how average the average person is. The American public is more concerned about the latest sluttery Miley Ray Cyrus is up to than that minor thing called "the national debt." Your average American would rather sop up whatever self-help swill Oprah writes than learn about the education bubble. And the simple fact nobody can pick up a copy of Reason magazine at the grocery store, but you can pick up any issue of People, US, the Enquirer, or Harlequin masturbation material is proof to just how mindlessly average the American public is. But before one perceives the above to be largely a female-dominated phenomenon, think again.

Because there can be nothing more average, more mindless, more meaningless than sports.

While Madonna is convincing 60 year old women they're still hot, 80% of the American men are glued to a TV set at a bar watching one large group of guys try to get a ball past another large group of guys in the all-so-important hopes of getting it past "the line."

Does world peace ensue if the ball gets past "the line?"
No.

Do we end world hunger if the ball gets past "the line?"
No.

Do we solve the mysteries of the universe, cure cancer, achieve immortality, or find out the meaning of life if the ball gets past "the line?"
No.

But that group of large guys with the *blue and white* jerseys got the ball past the line more than the group of large guys with the *red and orange* jerseys and that's worth spending at least 5% of our GDP on.

The truth is, there's nothing wrong with watching sports or enjoying a good game. But if it were only that. Sadly, millions of men (and women) pin their happiness and hopes, their actual mental state of mind, even their identity on whether or not "their" team wins. Severely average men spend hours sitting at Applebee's, eating wings, wearing some other man's jersey, chugging away light beers as they set up fantasy sportsball teams based on real athletes who don't even know (or care) that they exist. And while we mock the billions of women wasting their lives watching day time soap operas, vicariously living a fake life while pissing away theirs, there's just as many men wasting their lives watching pre-game shows, post-game shows, pre-pre-post-game shows, and calling into sports talk radio shows to Monday morning quarter-back men who are multi-million dollar professionals.

But the real tragedy is that despite TRILLIONS of human hours dedicated to these things, be it sports, celebrity gossip, or the slop served on TV, not one intelligent thing was ever said, nor one significant advancement ever made. It is a sad waste of human life that abnormally intelligent people just can't understand and, frankly, don't care to.

Envy

In my early 20's it was almost always a guarantee I would be the one NON-liberal or democrat at the multitude of house parties I would attend in Minneapolis. I say "non-liberal" because I was a libertarian, not a republican, but it took too long to explain the difference to a bunch of drunk 20 somethings. Still, I kept this dirty little secret to myself as I just wanted to go to these parties, have fun, and maybe take a girl home.

Unfortunately, it was almost always a guarantee that somebody would know me, know my dirty little secret, and in an attempt to impress a girl through a display of one-upmanship out me as the "dirty, nasty republican." Naturally, a large debate would ensue, usually the instigator leading the charge, but backed up by nearly everyone else at the party. The only problem was I was an economist, as well as a well-researched empiricist. And since the internet by that time had increasing amounts of economic data that could be looked up to confirm I was right, what originally started as a lopsided assault became a blood bath with me being the undisputed winner.

The problem is, even though I won, this made me very few friends. Usually after the debate ended (or people left in disgust calling me a fascist), very few people would talk to me, even fewer girls go home with me, when all I wanted to do was have a drink and get laid. And this is a problem abnormally intelligent people will get to deal with.

Envy.

The sad truth is some people will be envious of you simply because you're smarter. Not because you did anything wrong to them. Not because you insulted them or rubbed it in their faces. But just by the mere fact of discovery they find out that you are smarter than them or different. Of course, envy is natural, and perhaps even a good thing if it prompts you to take action to attain what other people have. Unfortunately, most people don't take this route and instead seem to be genetically compelled to view your superior intelligence as an insult, demanding a pound of flesh for the affront. And this demand manifests itself in many ways.

In school you are likely mocked or ridiculed, not so much as a nerd or a square, but rather somebody who unfairly benefited from luck. Forget you really had nothing to do with your IQ, and forget you might have actually worked hard in school. All of that is ignored and you are just deemed lucky. Their pound of flesh is usually paid either through ostracization, ridicule, the elimination of the honor roll, or simply taken out on you on the playground.

As you enter adulthood the envious don't get their "revenge" so much in the form of name calling or playground fights as much as they try to display their superiority in some trivial subject or another.

Displaying their knowledge of beer cases.
Talking about how their car is nicer than yours.
Bragging about their designer shoes.
The number of rock bands they saw in the 70's and 80's.
Making fun of your hair cut (true story).
Bragging about their career.
Or their supreme knowledge of sports.

It doesn't matter that you have no personal animosity towards them, or that maybe you even personally like them. Some people cannot brook that you are smarter than them and will insist they find something they are better at. This unfortunately results in a phenomenon where abnormally intelligent people are constantly being challenged to some kind of competition they never asked to be in, nor cared to win. It also proves to be a hindrance to socializing and making friends.

Even in the professional world petty jealousy and envy can lead to any number pitfalls, back-stabbings, or other hindrances to your career. People sabotaging your work. Office gossipers spreading rumors. Even your boss may handicap your career if he senses you're more intelligent than he is. Doesn't matter you could advance your division or your company to new heights. Doesn't matter that you have not one ounce of disdain for one person in the entire profession. There will be some people who identify your intelligence as a threat and will use work place machinations to undermine you.

There are other instances, but the larger point is envy is so deeply engrained in the human psyche it is guaranteed to present at least some problems in your social, educational, professional, and even dating lives.

Democracy

The natural consequence of envy is theft. And whether you like it or not, since we live in a democracy smart people pay this price. Of course, we obfuscate this fact behind a whole host of euphemisms and politically correct platitudes. But make no mistake about it, you will be the victim of theft due to your intelligence.

The reason why is for all the drawbacks of IQ, the pros do outweigh the cons. The smarter you are the more likely you'll enjoy a whole host of benefits. Mental health. Physical health. Longevity. Staying out of legal trouble. Stable nuclear families, etc. But arguably the most important benefit is financial. Smart people tend to be wealthier and make more money than dumber ones.

Unfortunately, because of the envious nature of humans and the fact we live in a democracy, this means society as a whole determines how much of your money and wealth you get to keep...and how much you're going to give them. And a cursory look at the state, federal, and local budgets show the majority of taxes (around 70%) is simply transferring money from smart people to dumber ones.

You may not like the politically incorrect nature of this observation, but it doesn't make it any less true. The majority of taxes are paid to bail out stupid people from their mistakes. Be it:

people on welfare who keep breeding children they can't afford or

bankers who were stupid enough to lend a 25 year old "Thirty-Thousand-Dollarnaire" $1.5 million to buy a McMansion

or (as I predict will happen)

bailing out students who took on $150,000 in student loans to pay for a "Masters in Pansexual Hispanic Ethiopian Musical Butterfly Studies"

abnormally intelligent people effectively pay a "smart person's tax" to pay for the mistakes of others in society.

The sting, however, is that the rest of society doesn't look at you and say,

"Thank you for sacrificing part of your finite life working up the money to shield me from the consequences of my idiotic mistakes."

They typically look at you as an "evil rich fat cat" who "didn't earn what he has" and "owes it to the rest of society" to "pay their fair share." At best this means the smart will forever be on the hook for less-intelligent people's mistakes, at worst a Stalinist-like purging of those "bourgeoisie bastards" who dared to be better than average.

Unfortunately, wealth transfers are the least of your problems. For in allowing everybody to vote, the genuine Idiocracy that ensues ultimately destroys society. Since everybody, smart or not, gets the right to vote *at best* you can hope for a government that is maybe competent. One that at minimum protects human rights, upholds the country's constitution, and maintains public services such as roads and defense. But what is more likely to happen is instead of genuine statesmen who are concerned about their stewardship of society, you get politicians and charlatans who only care about their political careers, and willingly lie to the population to get re-elected.

This undermines the long term integrity of a nation on several levels. The most common one is deficit spending where politicians of today borrow money against the future to buy votes from the constituents today. There is also bribery or lobbying where nothing but outright bribes are used by special interest groups to get preferential treatment over the population be it a corporation, fraudulent non-profits, or political party front-groups. And then there is group politics where politicians play off of people's innate tribalistic instincts, pitting them against one another to win them over as a voting bloc (minorities vs. whites, men vs. women, corporations vs. people, rich vs. poor, etc.).

Regardless of what tactic they use, ultimately, what they're doing is merely going after the largest and most easily duped voting bloc – not intelligent people. And they win over this voting block by doing three things:

1. Validating the mass' envy by providing some rationale as to why other people are doing better than them (blame group "x" for your problems).
2. Protecting their ego and pride so said people do not have to reflect upon or own up to their mistakes.
3. Bailing them out so they are effectively shielded from bearing the full costs of their mistakes.

This results in an environment where incentives are not only perverse and warped, but one wherein nobody learns from their mistakes. As far as they know, they didn't do anything wrong. Besides there were no consequences. Ergo, they keep on making the same mistakes, over and over again, completely unaware they're doing anything wrong, but with INCREDIBLE costs to society.

For example, the Savings and Loan bailout simply taught incompetent bankers they did nothing wrong and could recklessly lend as the government would bail them out. And while the Savings and Loan scandal of 1989 did not necessarily throw the US economy into the throes of a horrible recession, the *trillion dollar TARP bailout during the 2008 financial crisis certainly did*. But whereas we can point to other examples of how shielding people from their mistakes results in more perverse and damaging behavior to society at large, one behavior directly speaks to Idiocracy as it is primary determining variable of it:

Breeding.

The sad truth is smart people don't breed as much as dumb people. And while having dumb parents does not guarantee you will be dumb, there is a statistically significant correlation between IQ and fertility. Thus, by simple exponential math stupid people will outbreed smart people which ultimately guarantees a transition from a Democracy to an "Idiocracy."

In other words the society is becoming increasingly hostile to intelligent people. They are increasingly expected to not only bear the majority of costs of society's mistakes, but also because of envy to take the majority of blame. This not only provides a deterrence to working hard, excelling or achieving, but also heavily deters smart people from breeding. *"Why bring a child into this world?"* is an oft cited quote people with an IQ above 120 say because they at least know their theoretical would-be children would likely live in an even more insane and hostile world. Sadly, this results in a vicious downward spiral as there are fewer and fewer intelligent children, the only ones capable of producing the economic growth necessary to support society, and increasingly more less-intelligent, dependent children, incapable of supporting themselves, let alone society. Alas, the result will not be the oafish buffoonery displayed in the movie "Idiocracy," but rather the poverty that can be found in the trailer park, the ghetto, third world, or communist countries.

Eagles Surrounded by Turkeys

There are certainly many more examples, but the larger point is that Idiocracy is endemic to all of society. Every aspect of life is affected by it because society is defined by it. This does not mean your average person is an evil person out to get you, or that there aren't people with high IQ's making stupid life decisions. But that abnormally intelligent people are stuck in a world that is largely populated by, led by, and determined by people significantly less intelligent.

Certainly this can be mitigated by choosing the right friends, social circles, educations, careers, etc., but invariably, and especially in democracies, certain aspects of Idiocracy are inescapable. Consequently, this will limit your life in several regards. Direct financial costs in bailing people out from idiotic mistakes. Having to endure a mediocre, if not outright degenerate culture. Foregoing a family because you would love them too much to bring them into this world. Or simply the unsolicited envy of others.

But while these limitations in life are simple consequences of living in an Idiocracy, they focus on the by-products or environment an average population will create. The government, the culture, the psychology, the entertainment, etc. It doesn't focus on the people themselves. And this is the true tragedy and cost we face. For it's not only abnormally intelligent people who pay the price, but everyone.

As stated before, the only thing that matters in life is other humans. Not just because of family, friends, and loved ones, but because we have to interact with other people in society merely to get by. Simply because we have no other choice. Ergo, the cumulative intelligence of the population affects everybody in nearly everything. Our overall economic production and standards of living are determined by it. Our freedom and effective government also somewhat determined by it. Our life expectancy and mental health also heavily influenced by it. As well as our social, romantic, and emotional lives. And we can only be as great as the rest of society allows us to be.

This, perhaps, then leads to the nub of the issue and that is average people do not appreciate their lives as much and thus settle for mediocrity, thereby lessening the experience for everyone.

You could be on the verge of an economic theory that would eliminate poverty...
but most guys would prefer to watch the Packers take on the Patriots.

You could have the formula that would eliminate cancer...
but most women would rather watch the Hallmark Channel or read Salon magazine.

You could have had a brilliant epiphany about religion...
but your buddies would rather wait in line for a big screen TV on "Black Friday."

The vast majority of people are neither interested in, nor want to achieve greatness. The vast majority of people do not want to lead different or unique lives. They are perfectly content utterly wasting their time on a

mediocre life,
with a mediocre education,
with a mediocre career,
on a mediocre couch,
watching a mediocre sitcom.

The costs of this horrific waste of life cannot be calculated because it's theoretical. What would society look like if instead of pursuing pointless, meaningless endeavors such as reality TV, sportsball, and Bruce Jenner people aimed for excellence? Smart, average, dumb, what if people realized they were going to die, only had a finite amount of time of consciousness on this planet, and led their lives accordingly so? This is the true cost we all pay - what could have been. And what could have been was a lot more eagles soaring in society with a lot less turkeys anchored to the ground.

CHAPTER 3
EDUCATION

If the total costs of being abnormally intelligent were simply ostracization, alienation, increased taxes, Idiocracy, and envy, one could simply chalk those up to the statistical consequences of being the eagle surrounded by the turkeys. But as any high IQ person will tell you all of that pales in comparison to the pain, agony, torture, and suffering they, and millions of other young geniuses, endured every day during their childhood. And not just every day, but every day for AT MINIMUM 13 years. And that veritable gulag of mental torture is...

the "education" system.

The "Education" System

Let us be very clear.

The education system is NOT for the children.

It is NOT for the sake of education.

And it is certainly not for benefiting society or "our future."

It is a system designed to benefit teachers, administrators, unions, parents, and (less-so) employers.

The children are merely an afterthought, a vehicle by which others enrich themselves.

To understand why this scathing condemnation is not a condemnation at all, but an accurate assessment of today's education system, we need to go back to the origins of the US (and to a lesser extent other countries') educational system(s). These origins hail from the Prussian model of education which consists of compulsory, government funded education from the ages of 5 to 13. This model was advocated in the 1840's by congressman Horace Mann who was largely successful in revolutionizing the American education system to the Prussian one. Though originally Prussian in nature, it was adapted to fit the industrial revolution, teaching children obedience, punctuality, rote rehearsal, and other skills that would help them be successful workers in factories, plants, mines, etc. But while this model did certainly help employ students, provide labor to the burgeoning American industrial revolution, and increase standards of living for many, there were two main drawbacks to this system.

One, it did not teach individuality or excellence as much as it did conformance, obedience, and compliance. The ringing bells, the structured nature of the room, and the hierarchy of teacher versus students were purposely designed to make good workers, not good thinkers, innovators, or inventors.

Two, it's never changed in the 160 years since its implementation even though nearly everything else in the country has. In other words, it's completely outdated.

Take for example this picture of Oak Grove Middle School in Bloomington, Minnesota.

Do you see any oaks?
Do you see any groves?
Do you see anything that would inspire and excite the mind of a young genius?

Or do you see something that looks more like a prison than a school?

This is not coincidence in that many of the same principles that went into the Prussian model of schooling also went into the design of building prisons. Crowd control, lack of light/windows, and more recently zero tolerance policies, metal detectors, and even cops on campus. But the larger point is, even though there's certainly been some additions and reforms in the American education system, there has not been a fundamental revolution or restructuring from its outdated Prussian-Industrial model to optimize it to serve the educational needs of children today. And so instead of independent thought, creativity, innovation, and excellence they are taught...as were kids 160 years ago...conformity, compliance, and obedience.

The Hypocrites of Education

This environment is already bad enough for normal kids, let alone abnormally intelligent ones. But it gets worse. For whereas Horace Mann and teachers of 160 years ago very much had the best interests of the kids and society at heart, today the same cannot be said for those purporting the same thing.

Teachers for example are a laughably hypocritical bunch. How, at the age of 17, can you dare to declare an education major? How, when you're a mere four years into puberty with no real world, adult life experience decide you have the wisdom and experience to teach future generations? And how utterly pointless is it that you spent all this time in school to NOT spend any time in the real world, but merely, after a four year college degree, go back to the same system to regurgitate what you heard a mere short four years before from equally worthless "teachers."

The truth is the majority of teachers are not worldly, experienced adults but lazy adult children who fear math, rigor, and hard work. They mask their ulterior motive for an easy job with summers off behind the "noble cause" of "educating the children." But no matter how much they cowardly hide behind "the children" their true intentions still bleed through in the classroom and all students (smart or not) suffer.

With no real world experience their lack of passion for anything in life saps the life out of what would have otherwise been very interesting subjects. With no work ethic they don't take the time to consider how to keep their students motivated or interested because...well...that would take effort. And as they age their disdain for their students becomes ever more apparent as they become bitter, indifferent, and vindictive. The result is an environment that is once again more a prison than a vessel for learning.

Of course, none of this is improved with the ever-increasing bloat and overhead of NON-teaching staff. Diversity counselors, counselors, vice-principals, reserve vice-principals, nutrition directors, freshman coaches, JV coaches, varsity coaches, and let's not forget "tap and jazz" instructors. The fact spending per pupil adjusting for inflation has increased five-fold in the past five decades but with no significant increase in the academic performance of students is undeniable proof that the primary purpose of the education system is NOT the children, but an employment vehicle for some of the country's most worthless and talentless individuals.

And the parents. Ah yes, the parents.

The dirty little secret is most parents value themselves more than their children. And while they'll claim they had children under equally fabricated "altruistic" reasons, the truth is they had children first and foremost for themselves. Thus, for most modern parents, after six months of constantly having to monitor their infants, they tire of it, wanting nothing more than to outsource their child-rearing so they can get back to what truly matters in their lives – themselves. Their careers, masters degrees, nail appointments, happy hours, and daytime social clubs all, sadly, trump children in the real world.

You mix these ingredients together:

1. An outdated education system designed to mass-produce obedient workers
2. A talentless teaching staff incentived by money and laziness, not educating the children
3. An administration that further profiteers off of "educating the children" and
4. Indifferent parents who don't care about their children's education

and what you ultimately have is nothing that approaches an "education system," let alone one that allows truly intelligent kids to reach their potential. You have an over-bureaucratized, overstaffed, and overly-expensive baby-sitting operation used to house otherwise unemployable children during the day time so their parents can pursue their vanity while an entire industry of talentless charlatans make half a trillion dollars a year off of the child-chattel.

It is nothing short of prison for all children. But it is mental torture for those who are abnormally intelligent.

The 13 Year Prison Sentence

I had an interesting observation the last day of my compulsory K-12 education. There we were, waiting for the "final" bell to ring, and when it did the entire senior class went wild. They ran for their lockers, grabbed whatever it was they may have left in there. Banged on the tables and benches of the adjacent cafeteria, all screaming and yelling as they made for the door. It was as if the Allies had liberated Auschwitz and none of us would ever return to that hell hole again.

So tell me, what kind of system evokes such a visceral hatred and a desire to escape it?

Be it your senior year or just the last day of school when you were chomping at the bit to get out for summer vacation, no child,

and I mean NO child

liked school.

This was the odd insight I had because why wouldn't you like school? Why did this 13 year experience *HAVE TO BE* so tortuous and painful? Why did it feel like we were in prison? Why couldn't learning be fun? Why couldn't you make school a place young children would WANT to go to and one they'd HATE to leave, perhaps crying when it was over instead of celebrating its end?

The answer, as portended before, is because school is not intended for children and is thus a LITERAL prison for them.

When you take the US education system for what it is and in its entirety there is simply no denying that it is the epitome of child abuse and arguably the largest crime against humanity. You are taking the most innocent of people (children) who have neither agency nor command in their lives and compelling them to go to a place that is not designed for them, but rather others. Worse, you are robbing them of their childhood where 13 years of their youth will be pissed away on rote rehearsal, a subservience to others, and conformity culminating in a laughable façade called "education."

But whereas the majority of children do indeed view school for what it is (a prison), school is a particularly purified form of torture for those with a high IQ. Most students can at least adapt to the pure averageness and "lowest common denominator" traits of school, some even thrive. But for those students who are true geniuses school is the 10th and extra-special added bonus level of hell.

The Teachers are Dunces

First you have society's least intelligent adults teaching our most intelligent students. This is due to the fact that education majors and teachers tend to have the lowest IQ's out of all college majors. Admittedly some are smarter, some are dumber, but it's laughable to have an adult who is less knowledgeable and less intelligent than their high IQ students, teaching out of a book and a scripted lesson plan, trying to pass that off as "wisdom," "knowledge," and "education."

Unfortunately, it's worse as most genius students don't even know their teachers are for the most part a bunch of dunces. A third grader doesn't know their teachers are intellectually inferior people, only that they're "adults" and therefore superior. This misjudgment is the cause for a certain level of insanity as the child's intellectual superiority at times runs contrary to the authority of their teacher. Alas, the student could be right on...

a mis-graded paper,
a philosophical line of reasoning,
a political debate,
or some other aspect of education,

but if the teacher...

doesn't agree with him,
doesn't know the answer himself,
or frankly, just doesn't like the kid,

the student is punished, marked down, or told they're wrong.

This not only impairs the child's education, but is maddening for some students as what they **_know in their minds_** to be logical, truthful, and real is being rebuked by their teachers. It's not until they're older do they realize their teachers were wrong (about potentially scores of things) and the 10 years of confusion they suffered was completely unnecessary.

The Lack of Passion

A second drawback, which is related to teachers' intellectual inferiority, is that they lack the passion to make their presumed specialty interesting. I personally have taught both salsa dance classes and economics classes. And though one may be obviously more interesting than the other, it was my passion for both that made all my students equally interested, even excited about both.

Your average teacher, however, with their average IQ of 102 and a complete abhorrence of work, rigor, discipline, and excellence cannot possibly breathe the same level of passion, intrigue, and curiosity into their students' minds than a legitimate professional who absolutely loves their field. Furthermore, with no genuine mastery of the subject or real world experience most teachers are theoreticians, Monday Morning Quarterbacks, and academians. They merely got a four year education degree, avoided a real job in the real world at all costs, bringing nothing of experience, practicality, interest, or real life into their classroom. This results in an instruction style that can at best be described as going through the motions, and thus, like Ben Stein in "Ferris Bueller's Day Off," all of the students are falling asleep. Alas, it is **not the topic** that puts most students to sleep, but the **lack of passion** and practicality in the teacher that does.

Still, this doesn't change the fact the students aren't learning anything. If you think about it, nearly EVERY topic CAN BE made to be interesting. That is the job of the teacher. But if your teachers went into education because it's easy and "summers off" you can expect all your students to fight to stay awake in class, the high IQ ones, particularly torturedly so.

Rotten Apples Ruin the Lot

Third, while brilliant children are fighting to stay awake, let's not also forget another huge hindrance to their education. "Special ed" or "problem students." By lobbing the brilliant in with the average, you can expect a certain amount of efficiency loss as the brilliant must make accommodations to the average. But you throw in one or two ill-reared problem students, or more euphemistically called "special ed" students, and you can bring everybody's education to a screeching halt.

A bully starting a fight in class. An emotionally unstable child interrupting class. The class clown disinterested in his studies, and more obsessed with garnering attention. The single teenage mom whose drama overshadows history class. The list could go on, but the key drawback of the compulsory aspect of the Prussian education model is some children just should NOT be in school. And if you force them to attend, they are guaranteed to lessen the quality of education for every one else.

Problems arising from problem or special ed students, however, can be mitigated through the use of AP classes, special ed programs, and allowing for different tracks in education. But special education and the forcing of unfit children into school further belies the true motive of the education system. For while you would think teachers and staff would love to just get rid of all the problem students (or at least quarantine them), the truth is the education system LOVES problem students because of one simple thing.

Money.

While one competent teacher can educate 100, even 200 well behaved children, it takes an army of employees to control, let alone educate one problem student. Educational therapists, counselors, special ed teachers, special ed assistants, etc., an entire potpourri of ancillary staff is needed to babysit what amounts to nothing more than an inadequately-disciplined, misbehaving child. And so while your students may not like being throw in with the inmates (and the teachers certainly do not enjoy it either) it doesn't matter. There's a ton of money in having children unfit for school in the education system. And money trumps education, especially the education of abnormally intelligent children.

You Need Ritalin

But here another irony lies. What if you're not actually a problem student, but rather your teacher is particularly boring? What if he or she is particularly inept? And what if your brain is just too active and brilliant to tolerate the day to day mundanity 13 years of public education will bring? If you dare to act out, fall asleep, or perhaps (if you're a boy) take your pent up energy out on the playground you will get in trouble. But the truth is you're not a problem student, you're just bored.

Sadly, most teachers can't (nor really care to) tell the difference.

I remember a fellow classmate, John. He had an IQ off the charts. We were in a falsely-advertised class called "Creative Writing" which, upon attending, we realized was nothing more than a make-work program for our talentless English teacher, Ms. Leider. She had put no effort into the class. Couldn't care less about making the students passionate about writing. Certainly was not (and is not to this day) a published author on anything. And ultimately made something that could have been fun and intellectually rewarding, incredibly tortuous and painful.

John naturally revolted, not paying attention, talking in class and did the bare minimum to earn himself a C. Most other students rebelled in some fashion or another, doing the minimum and holding a grudge against the teacher who was wasting an hour per day of our finite lives. One day, inevitably John's behavior passed a line, prompting Mrs. Leider to yell,

"JOHN!!! I'VE LOST MY PATIENCE WITH YOU!!!!"

To which John responded WITHOUT MISSING A BEAT

"Sorry, but I can't help you find them."

At which point he was promptly sent to the principal's office.

The question is who was punished?

Certainly the teacher, in all of her infinite hypocrisy and inferiority, was not punished. She was the "adult." She was the "teacher." She was part of the system and therefore could not be blamed.

Naturally, therefore, it was the child. It was the student. It was John. Even though the root cause of this kerfuffle was his superior intelligence being unable to tolerate the ineptitude and indifference of the teacher. Ergo, John was sent to the principal's office and the teacher was likely paid a pension.

But that was 1991. The scary question is what would happen today?

Today, such an outburst of misbehavior and non-compliance would not just land you in the principal's office, but a recommendation you be put on Ritalin or some other mood-altering drug. Also, such a rebellious demonstration of superior intelligence would not be viewed as superior intelligence, but rather a mental problem. ADD, ADHD, Asperger's,

Autism, etc. This isn't to say these things don't exist, but they're all too conveniently used as an excuse to cover up teachers' inability to teach and blame it instead on abnormally intelligent children's natural frustrations with a mental prison.

Alas, prescription drugs and misdiagnosed mental disorders are another charming level of hell in today's education system.

You're Not Stupid, Just Bored

All of these costs, however, bad as they may be, pale in comparison to the two major and most costly prices abnormally intelligent people will pay because of school.

1. The loss of genuine education, and
2. Thinking you're stupid

Unless you had particularly involved parents who adamantly insisted on good grades, or perhaps were one of those rare few students who could actually pull off straight A's in this environment, the majority of brilliant children simply cannot tolerate school and mentally check out. This occurs when a high IQ student is inevitably worn down by the mundanity of school, ultimately loses interest in it, views it as a 13 year necessary evil, and writes it off completely.

This then sends brilliant minds into a catatonic or hibernated state. In order to survive and endure this pain, high IQ students expend the least amount of effort just to get by and keep their parents off their ass. They fall asleep, put off homework till the last minute, put forth the minimal effort, and day dream very much in a Calvin-and-Hobbes-like manner (you likely know somebody who said, *"I never did my homework, fell asleep in class, and still graduated with a 2.8!"*). However, the tragedy is while these students have checked out there are still good teachers in the education system who are brilliant at teaching and do indeed provide a valuable education to their students.

Too bad. It's already too late. The brilliant student has turned off his mind and is no longer receptive even to the most passionate of teachers and beneficial of classes.

This was my personal experience during high school. In hindsight my chemistry teacher was a brilliant man who did indeed teach with the passion of a Southern Baptist minister. But after four classes of History, English, Psychology, and Composition, all taught by charlatans posing as teachers, his passion and pertinence of chemistry could not stir my brain from hibernation. All his efforts and brilliance was wasted on my (and others') brains as we were simply too mentally beaten down to have the energy to care.

This, sadly, is a steep price to pay because in hindsight not only did I develop a personal interest in chemistry later as an adult, but it would have been a much better profession than the one I inevitably chose. I could have become a nuclear engineer, a physicist, or something else much greater than what I am today. This then behooves the question, how many potential Einsteins, Hawkins, or Jobs were lost to the doldrums of school? How many English teachers sapped how many future Ben Carsons' of their energy to study medicine? It's not just a price the individual pays in wasted potential, but what society lost out on in terms of what could have been had we actually educated our children.

The second tragic loss is the fact that school measures CONFORMANCE not INTELLIGENCE. Having a 4.0 means you're a great student, not necessarily a smart person. But very few, if any, young students know the difference. They assume good grades is the ultimate measure of your intelligence, and consequently what you can achieve in life.

Ergo, if you are getting C's and D's, you're not a brilliant young girl, cooped up in a mental hell hole.

You're stupid.

And if you're falling asleep in English class (because you already **read, write, and speak it fluently**), you're not a boy whose brain is being tortured with unnecessary pablum.

You're a moron.

In the end the young mind is fooled into misdiagnosing their true intelligence, thus underestimating their lifetime potential. You're not smart. You're dumb. You keep falling asleep in history class. You don't know what a diphthong is. You're too mentally spent to learn trigonometry. You certainly can't become a surgeon, a doctor, a quant, an engineer, or an entrepreneur! You can barely become a plumber! And don't even think about getting into Harvard or the MIT. That's reserved for smart people, not you. You get to go to community college, that's if they'll even have you. So enjoy your life of mediocrity, because that's all you are.

And so every year an estimated one million child geniuses underestimate their potential. They make lifetime decisions based on the false premise that they're stupid, which ensures they effectively waste their lives. They never challenge themselves, never knowing what they are truly capable of. They settle for careers and colleagues that are beneath them. Some are condemned to poverty when they were capable of riches. All the while foolishly thinking they're average or even dumb.

Thankfully, however, all of this is irrelevant. Because millions of teachers and school administrators got lifetime government jobs, overpaid pensions, and summers off. And that's all that matters in the world of education.

College

If it was 1955 the problems smart people would face when it came to education would end here. You would graduate from high school, land a job, maybe attend a trade school, and get on with your life. However, since 1955 the economy and labor market has drastically changed which ensures the abnormally intelligent pay one more pound of flesh when it comes to education. Specifically, college.

What has happened since 1955 is an effective educational arms race wherein increasingly more and more job seekers try to outdo one another by getting a superior education. This has had the expected consequences of flooding the labor market with college-educated job applicants, effectively making college degrees worth as much as 1955 high school diplomas. But further accelerating this arms race are two unfortunate facts about the US economy and labor market regulations.

One, the US economy today is growing 40% SLOWER than what it was in 1955. Whereas you could expect annual economic growth to average around 4.25% back then, today it is around 2.25%. This lower economic growth means less demand for employees making competition even fiercer in the labor market. This only forces more people to attend college, further lessening the value of college degrees.

Two, since 1971 IQ tests have been illegal to use as a means of employment screening and aptitude testing by employers. This means you cannot merely be tested for aptitude or intelligence and then get into a training program with an employer. You now (again) have to go to college, get additional training, and get a degree.

The overall effect of these economic and legal issues means not only are you more or less forced to go to college, but so is everybody else. And while back in 1955 college really was the preserve of smart people, today with everybody compelled to attend college *is* merely high school version 2.0. Alas, you get four more years of the exact same BS you did in high school, but this time you get to pay for it.

Lucky you!

High School v 2.0

I cannot emphasize this enough (because it's true)

COLLEGE IS HIGH SCHOOL VERSION 2.0.

Your parents will lie to you, your teachers will lie to you, your counselors will lie to you, all telling you the same thing;

"College is where the smart people are."

But it is a lie.

COLLEGE IS HIGH SCHOOL VERSION 2.0.

As a mentally-embattled and burnt out genius-student you will cling to college as this morsel of hope, desperately wanting to believe in it because you cannot endure another four years of the mental torture that high school was. You will want to believe it is the "promised land" where your classmates are as intelligent as you and you will finally be among your peers. You will also believe you will be able to *finally* study what you want, allowing you some command and control over your own destiny. But the education system is not through with you yet. Not by a long shot. And you are going to pay one final price.

First, by the fact everybody is going to college there is no longer anything special about it.

The idiot in your class who was picking fights with you on the playground?
Your lab partner for Freshman biology.

The ditzy cheerleader who talked in class incessantly?
Now a child-psychology major who also talks incessantly in your Econ 101 class.

The emo-kid who instead of genuine accomplishments in academics or sports tried to impress people by claiming he was a Marxist or an Anarchist in high school?

A pot head, spouting the exact same gibberish and is now your dorm mate.

Colleges, just like the K-12 system, is in it to make money. It is why only the elite schools reject people and nearly every other college doesn't. It's why you have remedial classes, even universities **setting up entire programs** specifically designed for flunk outs who couldn't even pass their GED's, all so they can inevitably be accepted into the traditional university and pay tuition. You combine this profit motive with the nearly insatiable demand for college degrees and colleges will let ANYBODY in.

In short, you didn't escape the idiots you hoped you left behind in high school. They all followed you and are going to make your next four years just as painful.

Second, any perusal of the class requirements to get a bachelors degree in any American university will quickly show you half of your classes will have nothing to do with your declared major. They will say this is to

"ensure you're a well rounded person" or
"give you a chance to explore" or
"make sure you get a diverse education."

BS.

It is to milk as much money out of you as possible.

When I taught economics at a culinary college the problem they faced was there was only so many stoves, ovens, and other expensive commercial kitchen equipment. This limited the number of students they could enroll and still effectively teach to become chefs. However, it dawned on them they could rent some nearby office spaces, mandate all students take some "pre-requisite classes," and then effectively have two shifts of students. During the day one shift would be using the equipment in the main building, while others would be taking their "required" classes in psychology, economics, and other hogwash. And at night they would simply switch. For the small price of renting a couple office spaces they not only doubled their enrollment but doubled the tuition students would pay with no measurable increase in their chances of becoming chefs.

Now while the school I taught at was a veritable degree mill, the same thing occurs at accredited ones. They don't want to turn you away, but they only have so much lab equipment or engineering professors for legitimate degrees on hand. Besides, they certainly aren't going to turn down any students stupid enough to major in "English," "Poetry," or "Chicano-Kangaroo Fluffy Bunny Studies" since all you need is a room, some chairs, and a washed up professor to teach. Ergo, just like a for-profit business, just like the K-12 education system, colleges' primary goal is to profit off of you. Unfortunately, whereas it was the taxpayers paying for your K-12 education, now it is you who gets to pay $200 a credit for classes you don't need and will do nothing to stimulate you intellectually.

The Faux Intellectuals

The final price genuinely intelligent people will pay in college is dealing with those who aren't. Specifically, faux-intellectuals. These are the idiots who aren't intelligent, but since they're on a college campus they desperately try to fake it. They fall into two general camps.

Your professors

and

college graduates.

Like K-12 teachers, most professors are worthless, talentless hacks who couldn't find jobs in the real world. They typically hail from enough parental money (or student debt) that they managed to get a doctorate or masters in their field. Unfortunately, most of the faux-intelligent professors majored in worthless subjects that required no intellectual rigor (the humanities, the liberal arts, etc.) so the only real place that will hire them is academia…to simply reteach what they learned 2-4 short years ago. This means you are guaranteed to run into them as you're forced to take their meaningless and pointless classes in "14th Century Lesbian Pygmy Sculpture" or "Diversity and Ethno-Centrism Privileged Studies."

The problem is, very much like your teachers being the "adult," you will assume your professors are smarter than you because…well…they're "professors."

Hogwash.

While there are certainly some professors who are authentic authorities and experts in their fields (predominantly STEM, engineering, the sciences, etc.) the majority of professors are like lawyers. At one time they were greatly respected, but now the market is flooded with them and so many are just avoiding real work, their title no longer carries any meaning.

Unfortunately, seeing them for the faux-intellectuals they are does not mean you won't suffer them much like you did most of your K-12 educators. The only problem is they're usually more sanctimonious, lecturing, and have some kind of political agenda to shove down your throat.
While the masses of average sheeple-students sop this tripe up, try your best to ignore it and placate your professors.

This then leaves you with your peers and fellow college graduates to suffer.

While in reality nearly anybody with a pulse can get into college, this reality never really dawns on the vast majority of average-intelligence people. Holding themselves to outdated 1950's standards, they actually think just because they were accepted into a college they are now somehow smart. And, therefore, whether they were studying "17th Century French Poetry" or "Transgendered Mozambique Turtle Studies" they deem themselves just as smart as you with your nuclear engineering degree.

It is here the price you pay has not so much to do with enduring these people on a day to day basis (because they're very unlikely to be in your Calculus III class), but when you deal with them in the real world.

I cannot tell you the number of couples I know where the wife has some fluffy bunnies MASTERS degree in education or communications while the husband has an average, ole boring BACHELORS degree in chemistry or petroleum engineering,

BUT

the wife still lords the fact she has an "advanced degree" over her husband insisting she's somehow intellectually superior.

This is but a microcosm of what you can expect to tolerate while you're in school (and out) as millions of genuine idiots who with a mere pulse managed to get a frivolous degree in some form of poppycock think they are intellectual equals to those who are genuinely intelligent. The woman with her "Masters in Philosophy" degree who can't shut up about it at a party while you clandestinely excuse yourself to the bathroom to avoid her averageness. The MBA braggart whose sole accomplishment is that he merely has his MBA yet no form of gainful employment. And the law graduate? The same, but with perhaps $50,000 more in student loan debt.

All of these genuinely intellectually inferior people are being dumped out into society in droves. And instead of pointing towards genuine achievements and accomplishments in life (of which there typically is none), they merely point to their increasingly-worthless sheepskins as not only validation of them wasting 20 years of life on a worthless education, but "proof" they are intellectually superior to you.

It isn't until they reach the age of 40, more likely 50, do they sheepishly admit their education does not equal intelligence. And even then most of them have nothing else to point to in life and therefore carry this meaningless Boy Scout Merit Badge to their grave as their single most important "achievement" in life. You get to pay a price as you indulge them in their life-long insanity.

CHAPTER 4
CAREER

Just because you escaped school does not mean you've escaped Idiocracy. Yes, school was an artificial environment you effectively spent your entire life under. And yes, school was inherently flawed in its design, execution, and staffing. But just because you're entering the real world does not mean people suddenly get their act together, let alone magically increase their intelligence. It's the exact same people you've always been with, now moving from college into the working world. In other words, Idiocracy is inescapable for abnormally intelligent people and it will, in one way or another, follow you to your grave. And the working world is no different.

However, since the working world is structurally different from school the "Curse of the High IQ" will haunt intelligent people in different ways. It won't be your teachers, but your bosses that are the source of your ire. It won't be students, but co-workers who slog down your progress. And instead of bus rides with rowdy classmates, it will be commutes with mindless worker drones. But what makes these problems particularly daunting is the fact that all the artificial supports you had in school are pulled out from under you. No longer will your parents or the government give/lend you money to pay for tuition, food, clothing, or insurance. No longer will your parents allow you to live at home during summer. And, oh, by the way, the government would like you to pay back those student loans now.

This introduces the added stress of finances, starvation, bankruptcy, and destitution into your life which puts you (at least early on in your career) in a highly desperate and disadvantageous position. You would think that all the work you put into school, being a highly intelligent person, and perhaps good grades would inoculate you against this, ensuring you have reliable and adequately-compensated employment. Unfortunately, it is not merely good grades, a hard work ethic, and intelligence that employers demand. Remember, the economy is growing nowhere near the rate it used to and there's millions of college-educated job hunters out there. This not only allows employers to be picky, but puts job hunters in a desperate situation. A desperation employers can smell.

To be blunt, today's American employers know they have you by the balls. You not only likely have student loans, but if you're like most Americans probably a car loan, some credit card bills, children, and a mortgage meaning you need your employer more than your employer needs you. And an unfortunate fact of life is that most people, when given power over others, become sadists and abuse it. So it's not merely "deliver A-level work" and "show up everyday," but a sick and twisted Twilight Zone of

Unpaid overtime,
Playing the "Read Your Boss' Mind" Game
"I don't have time to train you"
"It's a steep learning curve"
"You're not a team player"
"Personality adjustments"
Never ending CPE
"Kiss the Ring"
Pointless meetings

and whatever other demented psy-ops your intellectual-inferior bosses are going to wage on you.

Naturally, nobody likes this environment whether you're smart, dumb, or average. But like school the inanity, the pettiness, and the outright stupidity you are going to run into in the working world will be particularly long fingernails on a chalk board making you dream of the days you could go back to that prison called school.

Welcome to the working world.

<u>Finding a Job</u>

You can't endure the stresses of a job if you can't find one. And so, like everyone else, you get to enjoy rejection letters, cancelled interviews, rescinded job offers, promises to call you back, and more all while under the constant financial stress of not being able to make rent that month. But with luck, one of your resumes might get through. And if it gets through somebody might realize you're supremely qualified for the job. Matter of fact, you're PERFECT for the job! You're so perfect for the job they actually can't afford to lose you! And since most companies espouse the adage "employees are our best asset" they send out their very best assessor of talent....

the 23 year old HR ditz.

This scourge of the employment world, again, is nothing specific to abnormally intelligent people. *All people,* at one time or another, have sat across from a completely worthless, useless, clueless, 23 year old HR ditz and been pelted with questions that:

1. Have nothing to do with the job

2. Have nothing to do with your ability to do the job.
3. Make you want to reach across the desk and break her pretty little face

But it's particularly infuriating to abnormally intelligent people because it is an insult to their intelligence and all they've worked for. I've known petroleum engineers with 10 years' experience on oceanic oil platforms who endured the mockery of a 24 year old, math-impaired child who asked them "what's your favorite color and why?" I've known high-level network security experts who were forced to sit down and waste 30 minutes of their precious time being interrogated about "what their greatest weaknesses" were. And I myself, sat across from more than my fair share of HR ditzes who knew nothing of multivariable regression modeling, financial statement analysis, let alone simple addition, but still had the gall to ask me "where did I see myself in five years."

It's not only proof the employer is not serious about finding the most qualified candidate, but that they think so little of you and your accomplishments they send an adult-child emissary to assess your skills. Regardless, it's a blood-boiling insult abnormally intelligent people will have to endure.

"You're Just Not a People Person"

The HR ditz also introduces a new aspect of careers and the employment world. One that is the bane of existence for abnormally intelligent people.

"Soft" or "people skills."

In 2012 I had a job interview with a bank in Rapid City, South Dakota. I had not been this excited in nearly a decade in that Rapid City and the Black Hills area is my favorite place in the world, and I was now looking at the prospects of finally living there with gainful employment.

However, on my drive there I ran into the worst snow storm I have ever experienced in my life. Scores of cars were stuck in the drifts, at least five semi-trailers were in the ditch, and invariably it got so bad they closed the interstate down. It was only through some strategic driving, piggy-backing off of semi-trucks to plow through the drifts, and raw determination did I manage to make it to Rapid City. Unfortunately, I had not arrived until 4AM and only managed to get three hours sleep before my interview. I walked into my interview a bit fatigued.

The interview went very well and I even got the job in the end. But after receiving the job offer my future boss called me and said,

"We need to talk about something."

Curious as to what it was, I returned his call and found out he had a concern.

"Well, I noticed when you walked into the interview you weren't smiling. You see, we here at the Rapid City Bank want to give our customers an experience. And we need everybody to be smiling and happy to provide that warm welcoming environment. But when you walked into our office you were frowning and that kind of demeanor can..."

I cut him off and told him I was no longer interested in the job.

Whether it's a bank in South Dakota or a parking lot in Miami employers value "soft skills" or "people skills" more than real ones. And the reason is very simple. Normal and dumb people value feeling good over actual, genuine progress.

A perfect example is Oprah Winfrey.

Criticize her as you may, Oprah is a genius because she realized people would rather feel good than actually achieve good in their lives. And thus, she went out and told millions of women for over 20 years what they WANTED to hear, not what they NEEDED to hear.

You're not fat, you're beautiful inside!
Your husband should love you for who you are!
Follow your heart and the money will follow!
You deserve it girl!

For this she was rewarded billions of dollars in net worth.

The problem is high IQ people (unless they jettison their morals) simply can't do this which puts them at a disadvantage in the employment world.

First, they cannot keep up the charade or façade of emotional interest. It just isn't in their nature and it's simply too taxing mentally. High IQ people can plainly see a problem for what it is, what logical decisions need to be made in order to solve it, and can remove any emotional or psychological preferences they might have about it. They offer direct, blunt, emotionless solutions that are guaranteed to solve the problem, but unfortunately step on people's precious little toes.

This then leads to a second problem, because not only does the majority of clients prefer good feelings over production, but so too does the majority of co-workers and bosses. Your entire employment environment is driven by everybody's insistence you place feelings and emotions over reality and truth. This is simply maddening for smart people because what needs to be done in the real world counters what your boss, co-workers, and clients are demanding of you.

A colleague of mine worked at a video game store and was lectured for up-selling a client a $60 boxed-DVD set and NOT getting her to sign up for their membership card.

During my days in banking I was routinely lectured for being "too harsh" when analyzing and rejecting loans...until I was proven right when they all went into default and bankruptcy.

And no doubt you personally have experienced some instance of contradictory insanity in your own job where reality is telling you "X" and your boss is threatening to fire you if you don't do "Y."

It doesn't matter. Dumb and average people account for the majority of the customer base. Dumb and average people also account for the majority of workers at your firm. Thus, it is feelings and emotions that rule the day, guaranteeing you will suffer this cognitive-dissonance insanity during your entire career.

Third, there is some good news about people skills. Invariably, living in La La Land and not reality leads to the demise of the division, company, or entire industry. Wonderful as it is to live in the lies of emotions, feelings, and psychology, reality triumphs in the end. So while you may be driven insane by society forcing you to develop your ~~lying~~ "soft skills," in the end you will be proven right.

The most ardent acolytes of Oprah of the 1990's are the old, miserable, divorced and lonely women of today.

The housing bubble not only burst, but took the heads of nearly every boss I ever worked for in banking.

And the video game branch my buddy worked at got shut down because of turnover.

There's just one minor problem.

If you're right, and reality does rear its ugly head, that means your branch, division, or entire company will go under. And if it does, it will take everybody with it, even the Mythical Cassandra's like you who tried to stop it.

Alas, even though it is incredibly painful it makes a compelling argument to perhaps just sell your soul, kiss ass instead of kick ass, and try your best to hone your "people skills." Practice your "soft skills," learn to "network," lie and tell people what they want to hear. No employer is going to be any better than another and you just make it worse for yourself if you insist on some level of excellence or achievement. Remember, these are average people where "feelings uber alles" and nothing is going to change that.

Co-Workers

While it's already established the majority of people you will be working with are average or dumb and will insist on feelings over reality, it does not address the specific issues you'll run into when it comes to your co-workers and bosses. And here a whole new world of pettiness, pointlessness, and stupidity will come in, reminiscent of those fun times back in high school.

Thankfully, however, when it comes to co-workers there is really nothing new than what you already endured in high school and college before. If anything it's better in that these people now have to obey and conform (if they don't wish to be fired), plus they're in the same boat as you when it comes to today's desperate labor market. This isn't to say co-workers can't make your life a living hell with office politics, drama, ineptitude, procrastination, even sabotaging your work. But merely keeping a low profile, staying out of office drama, and keeping work separate from pleasure will minimize most of these problems.

The real problem abnormally intelligent people will run into during their careers is without a doubt going to be their bosses. And the reason is simple. Co-workers are not in the position of power to control, manage, limit, manipulate, or obstruct you and your progress in your career. They cannot serve as a road block to your career, capping what your intellect can achieve. However your bosses most certainly can. And unless they're also abnormally intelligent, it is a guarantee you and your bosses are going to ram heads in the future.

Bosses

In order to understand why nearly every abnormally intelligent person rams head with management you need to understand how one advances in business, employment, and careers.

Conformance, not performance.
Compliance, not excellence.
Ass kissing, not ass kicking.

The reason is in part found in what we previously discussed - that it is human nature to value feelings and emotions over reality and performance. But more so it is found in the structure and nature of businesses, namely one of efficiency.

In short, you can't have a bunch of leaders, executives, managers, and vice presidents staffing a company. Matter of fact for any organization (business, military, school) the vast majority of your employees need to be workers and not managers. If they're not, then nothing actually gets done and the entity either fails or goes bankrupt.

Because of this the structure of most businesses (or any large organization) is a handful of people up top developing the overall strategic plan and disseminating that plan down through their lieutenants and mid-managers to the employees or ground troops below. In order for this plan to work everybody has to do their part, and in theory the overall executive strategy will be a success.

But notice where the emphasis is put in this type of employment structure. Your value as an employee is not how intelligent you are, or if you "think outside the box," or if you come up with a revolutionary way to streamline a process. It's simply whether you're compliant and do your job. And not just do your job, but do it the way you were told AND preferably without asking too many questions. In other words, obedient, compliant, COMPLETELY AVERAGE people, especially those with ~~ass-kissing~~ "great people skills," thrive in this environment and are the ones who get promoted and become bosses.

This coincides then with a concept called "The Peter Principle." The Peter Principle simply states people are promoted to their level of *IN*competence. For example, say an average worker does what he's told, doesn't think about any of the underlying machinations of his job, and is just a good foot soldier. Because of his compliance his supervisors deem him worthy of promotion and he is promoted to Assistant Manager. After a couple years here, again, he is a great and obedient worker bee. He questions nothing, really doesn't contemplate the inner workings of the firm, but does what he's told, tells people what they want to hear, and he is promoted to Manager. Here, again, he excels at his job, merely doing what he's told, being a good, obedient worker. But, unfortunately, when he's promoted to Regional Director he is promoted beyond his competencies. He doesn't know how to sell. He doesn't know how to do marketing or demographic analysis. He can't read financial statements. He is a fish out of water and cannot do his job. Therefore, he is promoted no further, staying there as a dysfunctional, incompetent boss to which scores of employees must answer to.

In other words because of the structural nature of companies, combined with humanity's preference for feelings and emotions over reality, it is NOT the smartest or best people who get promoted, but rather the most average. Worse, when you consider The Peter Principle, these average bosses are promoted to the point of incompetence, not only threatening the integrity of the company, but making their employees' lives a living hell.

However, as is typically the case with abnormally intelligent people, this is a particularly grinding hell.

For there is nothing more frustrating than having your future potential in the hands of an intellectual inferior who is an incompetent boss to boot. And so the challenges high IQ people are going to have with their bosses will fall into roughly three categories. The first of which is just genuine incompetence and a lack of leadership on the part of your boss.

Leadership

True leadership, true and genuine leading requires intelligence, an independent mind, the ability to delay gratification, the ability to think long term, and above all else a spine. For example a true visionary would look at today's technology and ask a question I've been asking myself for about five years...

Why do we commute anymore?

The technology has existed for nearly 10 years that nearly every white collar office worker could work from home. Not only would this eliminate rush hour traffic, but it would add two hours a day of free time to be spent with family and loved ones per working parent. Not only would that lead to happier and more stable families, but less divorce, less crime, less poverty, and better grades. It would also save the government HUNDREDS of billions in highway maintenance, not to mention corporations HUNDREDS of billions in unnecessary office expense. It would be the single largest advancement in society since the personal computer.

But the reason the entire country is forced to endure a daily commute on traffic-jammed roads is because instead of real leaders we have millions of compliant, obedient, and incredibly average bosses who are not intelligent enough to get past the third grade quandary of

"Well, if I can't see you then how do I know you're working?"

Alas, the entire country is held hostage by a bunch of Peter-Principled, MBA-laden idiot commoners because they don't understand telecommuting.

Regardless, the example above highlights the difference between a REAL leader and your everyday, common boss. A real leader, a real boss is trying to make genuine advancements and achievements to not only benefit the company, but himself, and society. He or she looks beyond mere compliance and has a genuine intellectual interest in how to not only make things better, but dramatically better. It is these types of bosses that high IQ people can work for in that your brain will be intellectually stimulated and challenged.

Your average boss, however, comes nowhere near this. He is usually so incompetent, so average, and so obedient his "leadership" strategies entail the same tiresome tactics that have never worked in the past 50 years:

Meetings
Motivational posters
Motivational speakers
More meetings
Corporate retreats
Meaningless plastic trinkets as rewards (Wells Fargo is a perfect example of this)
Meetings about meetings
Continuing Professional Education
And whatever other pablum endorsed by the latest "business management" books.

In short, you may not personally hate your boss. He or she could be a great person. But even if they are personable, you will at minimum be limited to their ability to lead and achieve. And the truth is for every genuine leader that is out there, there's a thousand everyday, average, incompetent bosses who don't know they're the butt-end of Dilbert's Pointy-Haired Boss' jokes.

Intimidation and Insecurity

If you can't have a genius leader as a boss, the best you can hope for is a "nice" average boss. Unfortunately, human nature being what it is, and average people being who they are, it is much more likely your standard "average boss" will not view your intelligence as an asset to use and deploy, but rather a threat. They will be intimidated by your intelligence.

At first I believed this was just what disgruntled employees said about bosses they hated. How could somebody be intimidated by a subordinate's intelligence? Do bosses REALLY worry about some young whipper-snapper outshining them to their boss? Additionally, why wouldn't a boss want to use a smart employee's intelligence for the advancement of the company? However, this erroneously assumes some kind of idealism or superiority about bosses. That they're not only moral, intelligent, and wise, but also somehow hail from a better caste of society different than ours and therefore would never resort to such pettiness.

BS.

Bosses are cut from the exact same moral societal cloth we all are and are humans just the same. They have the same weaknesses, desires, urges, thoughts, fears, and flaws as anybody else. They are no better, wiser, or smarter than any of us, merely older. And like everybody else they are driven first and foremost by self-preservation.

What the average abnormally intelligent person does not see is just what a threat their intelligence is to organizations and those who run them. Specifically, a truly intelligent person easily identifies inefficiencies, flaws, and ways to drastically improve the system or organization in front of them. While through innocent eyes this seems to be the only logical and moral thing to do (not to mention profitable), in being so efficient, perhaps even revolutionary in your thinking, you unknowingly obsolete entire branches, divisions, subsidiaries, even companies...and all the employees and bosses employed by them.

For example, I had programmed a financial analysis model many years ago in 1996 to help with an accounting class I was taking. Over the past 20 years I used it in nearly every job I ever had, tailoring it to specific purposes, adding bells and whistles as needed. In its final form it was fully capable of automating the entire underwriting and loan-approval process for around 90% of the loans in the banking industry and for $1/40,000^{th}$ the cost of any comparable software out there.

So why was it like getting a cat to take a bath when I tried recommending it be implemented at the banks I worked?

At first I thought it was laziness. Many of my baby boomer bosses were (frankly) too lazy to learn Excel and simply insisted on using their old MS Word templates, doing the financial calculations by hand. Some of my bosses complain about aesthetics. They didn't like the "font." The charts didn't "look the same." Even the color of the lines they found fault with. But the real answer was this model streamlined so much of the underwriting process it would render nearly 90% of the commercial banking staff obsolete. And these guys knew it.

It wasn't until I was at my last employer did I realize what I had in my hand and why there was such resistance to my simple, 20 year old Excel model. By the time I left I was doing ALL the underwriting for ALL the bankers in ALL of the branches. That was one man doing the work of 12. And while I thought this would bring value to the company, cutting their underwriting expenses by 92%, that value would not be realized until they laid off the deadweight, supervisors and managers included. And they weren't about to do that.

In other words, truly intelligent people tend to be creative, innovative, and efficient people. So creative and efficient they sometimes directly threaten the personal and inefficient fiefdoms various incompetent bosses have built for themselves over the years within a larger organizations. So when...

a sharp budget analyst discovers 30% bloat in the government program budget,
an economist programs a model that does the job of 100 men, or
Shawn Fanning programs NAPSTER

then...

the program director fires the analyst
the economist is never promoted, perhaps demoted and lectured, and
the entire recording industry goes into a lawsuit frenzy.

Remember, bosses are average people, with every day average problems, and everyday average work ethics. They have debts they can't afford, wives about to divorce them, a boss who also hates them, and like most average people are lazy. They'd rather fight tooth and nail, avoiding change to protect their outdated fiefdoms than let some hot shot, intellectually-superior subordinate obsolete or steal their job.

And that is why they are deathly afraid of you.

Sadism

If incompetence and insecurity wasn't enough to deal with, enter in good ole fashioned sadism. Because as stated before, when you give people power over others, unfortunately most of them become sadists. And it is a guarantee you will run into these inferior, worthless pieces of human scum who through deceit, lies, manipulation, or just dumb luck will manage to become your boss.

Remember that model I programmed 20 years ago?

Since that time it had grown from a relatively simple model to a rather complex and complicated one with well over 300 formulas and calculations. Of course, I had 20 years to test and perfect the model so I was not worried about its integrity.

But "Paul" was.

Paul had come from a much better bank than the one I was currently working at. It was also a lateral move for him in that he was a VP there and was now going to be a VP here. It didn't make sense. Why would he willingly jump ship from a superior bank to one that was about to go bankrupt?

It soon because apparent. He was a clinically anal-retentive control freak and nobody could work with him for long...including his previous employer.

I don't know how, but he immediately pegged me as the largest threat in all of the bank. And he was right. While he intimidated most people, I couldn't care less about him. I was already planning on leaving once I got my bonus, he wasn't my direct supervisor, plus people like him made me want to intentionally aggravate them. So when I didn't buckle under his various nuanced intimidations, he had it out for me. And he was going to "prove" it.

The problem for Paul though is that I'm not sloppy in my work. I'm a professional. And I'm also smarter than he is. But worse for him is he picked what was arguably my most tested and proven piece of work in my entire life – my 20 year old model.

During an executive meeting he made an announcement that he had found a "glaring" mistake in my model. I raised one eye brow because I was genuinely curious, but not worried as to what possible mistake he found. But in the end he was right. There was a "mistake." The "Quick" and "Current" ratios were calculating the same number even though they were (GASP!) *not, in fact, the same ratio.*

Never mind this was a very minor mistake. And never mind none of our analysis really depended upon the quick or current ratios. All I did was point out one, simple, minor fact.

"Paul, you told me you wanted those formulas changed. I changed them to your specifications yesterday."

There was silence from across the table.

The larger point of the story is not that Paul was made to look the psychopathic idiot he was. Nor is it to belabor you with yet another story of my model. The point is in order to find this flaw one would have to spend AT LEAST six hours sifting through all the formulas and code to find it, which Paul most certainly did. Combine this with the fact he thought the quick and current ratios not matching were worthy of bringing up in an executive meeting, and it proved one thing;

Paul was just another mentally ill, sadistic boss to be thrown into the heap with the others.

There was Jessica the senior economist (at a very large bank) who would hold me hostage for hours in her office as her personal therapist while I was trying to work as an intern. I'd hear about her dating life, how she wanted a Latin lover, and all of the problems of moving from LA to Minnesota.

There was Hector, the egomaniac trust-fund baby from Hong Hong whose dad would finance his various dotcom ventures, none of which were business concerns, all of which were hobbies. He would throw temper-tantrums in the middle of the office, screaming at employees when they asked what he wanted them to do as it interrupted his "playing make believe CEO" where he'd hold pointless meetings and book unnecessary flights to China.

And Pete. Pete who kept screaming at me to ignore all the massive losses on one of our client's income tax statements, accusing me of not being a "team player"....until the FBI called him and told him our client was under investigation and they would very much like to see all of our files on him.

I could go on, but the point is sadism is much more rampant among the managerial classes than you'd like to think. And if you think it's difficult dealing with an incompetent boss, afraid you might "steal his job," just wait till you deal with the sociopaths out there who purposely enjoy torturing their employees.

But if you really want to incur the wrath of sociopathic bosses, if you really want to set them off and see just what kind of hell they're capable of, you just have to do one simple thing.

Be smarter than them.

And heaven help you if you are.

The reason why is like most average bosses, sadistic bosses lack the intelligence, work ethic, or temerity to get ahead. But whereas average bosses get ahead through almost mindless conformance, sadistic bosses get ahead through manipulation, deceit, lies, and outright immoral behavior. They are always running a scam. Because of this they're always on the lookout for people who are capable of outing them for the charlatans they are. And usually those are people who are smarter than them. Alas, it is no coincidence Paul made a bee-line for me, Jessica held me hostage in her office, Hector went into weekly tirades, and Pete was constantly threatening to fire me. All of them deep down inside knew I knew they were posers.

But the problem was I didn't know, at least not when I was younger. All I knew was what I knew in high school and college;

Jessica was older and superior to me. Therefore, she must know what she's doing.

Hector was the CEO and owner of the firm. I had to listen to him and besides, maybe I was a lousy employee for not reading his mind.

And Pete, well he was 55 and worked in banking 30 years. I *must have* overlooked something because a man with that level of experience can't be wrong.

It didn't dawn on me these people were horrendously incompetent supervisors, not to mention mentally ill sociopaths.

Alas, it is very similar to having a controlling boyfriend or abusive parents. The abusive boyfriend/parents deep down inside know they're the abusers. But they can't let the abused know that and need to keep them in the dark. Therefore they blame everything on the victim, claiming it's their fault.

"You're not working hard enough!"
"You're too stupid to know what you're talking about!"
"I'm the boss and what I say goes!"

Sadly, the employee, much like the girlfriend or the children, simply doesn't know it's not their fault and that it's the boss/boyfriend/parents who has the problem. And the sheer insanity that ensues as you vainly try to make the abuser happy, changing yourself when you weren't the problem, only to be punished again is maddening.

Of course, the only solution is to walk away, but drawing another parallel between abusive relationships and abusive employers, the victim is usually financially dependent upon their abusers in some way. Children need their parents for money. The girlfriend needs the boyfriend for rent. And the employee needs the sadistic boss for food. And most sadist bosses know this.

Unfortunately, it's not until a game-changing event like a housing bubble bursting, an FBI investigation, or the company going under do you realize these sick, sadistic vermin for what they are. The only thing you can do is be smart enough to identify them early on and if you can, as in the case of Paul, show them down, threaten them with legal action, go over their heads, record conversations, and be willing to get fired and collect a government check before suffering under such scum.

No job is worth the abuse.

The Only Careers Geniuses Can Really Have

The truth is most abnormally intelligent people cannot work under average bosses, and they certainly cannot work under sadistic ones. Their brains just can't tolerate the average, let alone, abusive employment relationships that account for nearly all the jobs today. And they certainly cannot "look busy" for six hours a day because they did all their work in two. This unfortunately relegates most intelligent people to three forms of employment.

High demand jobs
Entrepreneurship, and
"Minimalism"

High Demand Jobs

If you still insist on some sort of traditional structure in your life where you go to school, get a degree, and then get a career, you simply cannot go to an average school, get an average degree, and then get an average career. Your brain will not be stimulated enough, your working environment will not allow you to achieve your potential, and you will be stuck in the hell previously outlined in this chapter. You need to enter fields that are so specialized and in such demand you essentially are your own boss and can dictate your own terms.

Unfortunately, this means fields that require intense schooling in the most difficult of subjects. Engineering, IT, computer science, medicine, pharmacology, geo-engineering, dentistry, etc. In short, you have to find the most difficult degrees out there, spend your youth getting them, more often than not going to grad school, and then, upon graduation being one of the few 20 somethings who can honestly say to employers,

"You need me more than I need you."

Still, even if you go this route there is no guarantee you won't run into HR, you won't have to suffer incompetent co-workers, or won't have a sadistic boss. You may be able to walk away from an abusive employer or an intolerable working environment, but you'll still have to find another employer and are therefore perpetually dependent upon them. Because of this, it is my humble opinion the *only* form of employment for abnormally intelligent people is self-employment or entrepreneurship.

Entrepreneurship

In being your own boss you have the number one luxury of...

having no boss.

You call the shots, you make the decisions, and you get to run your company how you see fit. This is ideal for the abnormally intelligent in that there are no limitations, hindrances, anchors, or hurdles to what you want to do. If you come up with a brilliant idea there are no meetings, presentations, cajoling, or lobbying for it to get implemented. You simply *do it*. If you see a problem that needs immediate fixing, you fix it. No sounding the bells, tolerating office politics, worrying about obsoleting some mid-manager's fiefdom, and maybe getting authorization from the higher-ups to fix it. It's fixed. This not only allows for a much less-stressful working environment, but a much more efficient one since the single largest obstruction to your success and advancement (your boss) does not exist.

Of course, many people may not want to become entrepreneurs or don't think entrepreneurship is for them.

Tough. It's sadly coming to the point you have no choice.

When you consider the mental pain and suffering you'll endure as a smart person in today's corporate America, not to mention how it is nearly impossible to achieve anything near your potential when working for someone else, entrepreneurship (whether you want to become one or not) is pretty much the only choice. Furthermore, the belief that traditional employment is somehow more "stable" or "reliable" is laughable. This is not 1948 where everybody loyally works at the same factory for 20 years and retires with a pension. Employers will lay off thousands if it means an added penny to the bottom line. File for bankruptcy if it means they can jettison your pension. And move jobs overseas if it saves a nickel. Ergo, self-employment is infinitely more stable than traditional employment in that you are the most loyal person to yourself.

Of course, this doesn't mean you become an entrepreneur overnight. Nobody graduates from college and "POOF" magically starts a successful business the next day. But your primary long term career goal should be one where you employ yourself. Certainly work in an industry to develop an expertise and some skills. Certainly work in a profession to save up some money, maybe buy a house, and get yourself some seed capital. But you cannot rely either financially or mentally on today's modern employers as a source for reliable, long term, and meaningful employment. They simply do not exist in an Idiocracy.

Minimalism

Finally, if you don't want to go to school for 10 years to become a surgeon, nor want to waste your efforts on entrepreneurial ventures that may or may not succeed, the path of minimalism is the final "career" choice for the abnormally intelligent. The concept of minimalism is simple. You eliminate your need for money to the maximum extent possible, thereby eliminating the need for an employer to the maximum extent possible. This may not lead to a life of riches or material wealth, but it isn't intended to. It's designed to lead to a life of freedom where you answer to no one and do what you want when you want. This presupposes you have little to no desire for material things and are happiest with the company of others, a book, or other forms of mental (and free) stimulation. It also assumes your jobs won't be anything rewarding, but will be simple and stress free (janitor, security guard, stock boy, truck driver, etc.). It certainly may not be the life your capable of, but it sure as hell beats what most people have.

CHAPTER 5
SOCIALIZING, DATING, AND MARRIAGE

Socializing

For all the drawbacks there are to school, there is one incredible benefit. They congregate a critical mass of young people together in one spot. At first this may not seem like such an incredible benefit. Cliques form, fights ensue, mental trauma is suffered, and childhoods are wasted. But in this gulag-like morass of public education high IQ children enjoy something they will never again upon entering adulthood – enough high IQ peers to form a social life.

If you think about it school is the only time in one's life where all the children within the region are forced to go to the same place and socialize. And while there is everything wrong with today's education system it does bring a critical mass of all types of children together. This creates the environment where friendships, some of them life-long, form which is one of the most important things a human can have in his or her life.

Of course, high IQ children are likely to be mocked as geeks and nerds.

And yes, abnormally intelligent children will get beaten on the playground.
And yes, genius children will be mentally tortured by their teachers for 13 years.

But in the end they meet equally-intelligent peers who are so statistically rare, it would be unlikely they'd ever meet and form friendships had there been no such thing as school.

Unfortunately, school is an artificial environment and once college is done, this artificial environment goes away. And what children (who are now adults) assumed was going to be a constant variable in their lives since the age of five and would continue on forever...ends. And slowly, but surely so too does the number one thing in their lives – their friendships.

This presents the fundamental problem high IQ people face in their social life. What they considered to be a "base" or "normal" social life is not sustainable. It is very much like a stock market bubble, pumped up by temporary forces that will inevitably go away. And when these forces go away (school and college) their social life will "crash" down to where it should be or is considered "normal."

However, the social life that is considered normal for an average person with an average IQ is NOT the same for an above-average person with an IQ of 135. Remember, 68% of the population falls within ONE standard deviation of an IQ score of 100. This means the average Joe can go down to the bar and likely find scores of average Joes equally excited about sportsball and swingystick. But if you are two or (heaven help you) three standard deviations above average less than 1% of the population is at or near your intellect. This sheer rarity of smart people makes having a social life incredibly difficult. It's not only hard to find equals, but nearly impossible to find them in the quantities needed, *LET ALONE NEARBY,* to have an effective and rewarding social life. Thus, the crash from the artificial social life supported by a fleeting school environment to the base or normal social life supported by the real world is cripplingly dramatic for abnormally intelligent people.

But what makes it worse is the rate at which it happens.

Unlike a stock market crash a smart person's "social life crash" does not happen within 15 minutes of trading for reasons that are readily identifiable. It is amortized over a long, painful, and confusing process that can sometimes last over two decades. Worse is because we were so normalized at a young age to think the inflated social life school afforded us was normal we have no idea why our social lives are collapsing, and become increasingly distraught as our efforts fail to stop it. One day you were out partying with your buddies in college, now you're contemplating buying a fifth of scotch to make your day go by faster, and you have no clue why.

However, if we take the time to understand why this is happening and identify the various stages of "attrition" that occur in our social lives, it won't necessarily solve the problem, but it will at least provide sanity...not to mention serve as a warning to younger high IQ people as to what their future holds.

Attrition

The first stage of attrition starts the day you leave school for good. This could be high school, college, grad school, even the military. Once you leave any artificial environment where abnormally high numbers of similarly-aged peers are congregated together you have left the environment that has been producing the abundance of raw materials that has made your social life.

You replace this then with a career. And when you do, two things happen.

One, you are no longer attending a place with similarly intelligent people you choose to hang out with and socialize with. You are thrown into a petri dish of commoners, none of which you have the same rapport you did with your buddies in school, and

Two, your buddies are doing the same.

At first this may seem to be a boost to your social life. You are no longer burdened with the unnecessities of school and can now focus on work and making money. Additionally, you can spend your early 20's traveling, going out drinking, partying, gaming, or whatever it is you dreamt of doing while cooped up in college. This certainly will be a boost to your social life, but only in quality, not quantity. For if you were paying attention you'd realize that the handful of friends who took jobs out of state was the single largest decrease in your social network since you started school in kindergarten. Sure it may have been two or three guys who joined the military. And so what if it was just a couple girls who left the group to pursue their careers in New York? Yes, it certainly was innocuous. But it's the beginning of the end.

The next stage of attrition comes with the opposite sex. Not that you were unaware of them up until now, but some of them (namely women) want to start having babies. Some of them even want to get married before doing so! Of course, the courting process takes a bit which may grant your social life a bit of a reprieve, but your friends (male or female) do not have to get married before they're picked off like German Messerschmitts in the Battle of Britain ne'er to see their friends again. All it takes is one cute boy or one cute girl to whisk away your best buddy and suddenly he's "too tired" or she's "staying in" to grab a bite at the local Perkins.

This stage of attrition is about twice that of the first and accelerates over time. Soon your ranks drop down 25%, 30%, perhaps even a full half as your friends find significant others and prefer their company over yours. Of course, their intention was never malicious, as if you had somehow wronged them and they never want to see you again. It's just the facts of life that biology is the single largest force in the human psyche and friends are inevitably trumped by sex, love, and pair-bonding with the opposite sex. You may not like this, but it is a fact you do not control.

Still, even though they're spoken for you do manage to see your friends. Less frequently of course and not for those nightly romps around the dive bar district, but still maybe once every two weeks, perhaps once every three. Even marriage doesn't stop this as marriage is merely putting a governmental rubber stamp of approval on a relationship that already exists. Rings or not, your buddies still hang out, your girlfriends still have girls' night out, and your social life isn't totally crippled yet.

That is until...children.

Children are the third and most devastating stage of attrition to your social life. And the reason why is because it has to be. When people have children they (should) give up their current life to ensure their children are properly raised in theirs. And while your friends' breeding may be the death knell to your social life, it would be the epitome of child abuse if they prioritized their social lives over their children.

Children, however, present a two sided coin when it comes to the social lives of abnormally intelligent people. One, you certainly don't have to be on the receiving end of this to have your social life ended when it comes to children. If you yourself have a child your social life is just as effectively over as if all your friends were to have children. But, two, smarter people tend to have less kids anyway. Their reasons are many and valid, but it doesn't change the fact that this more or less forces them to endure the attrition of their social life as their friends follow their biological imperative, and they don't.

In other words, you're in a catch 22. If you have kids your social life is effectively over, which is fine because presumably this opens a new chapter in your life (a family) and replaces your proto-family (your friends). But if you don't, there is nothing to replace your slowly crumbling social life because, once again, you didn't join the "herd" and breed. And since friends were all the family you had and humans are the most important thing in life, this stage of attrition is particularly painful.

This then leads to a fourth stage of attrition. And not so much attrition, but rather ostracization. By the time you're in your 30's and assuming you had no children, you are statistically likely to be doing very well and start substituting adventure and exploration for the increasing absence of friendship. This is a double edge sword in that you increasingly lead a much more interesting and engaging life, but with fewer and fewer people around.

You want to go sky diving in Madagascar?
Very interesting, but your friends can't afford it.

You want to learn to tango in Argentina?
Fascinating story and an amazing experience, but your buddy's wife is having another child.

How about climbing Mount Kilimanjaro?
I would love to, but I haven't kept in shape like I used to in my 20's. The hike would kill me.

This results in a vicious spiral wherein substituting an increasingly adventurous life for a social one further removes you from whatever social circles you had. You could have visited the Arctic Circle, done the Beartooth Motorcycle Rally, visited the ruins of Sudan, but there you are at the exact same Christmas party with the exact same stories and exact same observations about the exact same topics every Christmas party conversation ever was.

"My child is four but reads at a 7th grade level!"
"I really need to finish my masters, but my company won't pay for it."
"My goodness, did you try the cake!? It's EXCELLENT! I need the recipe!"
"I really need to hit the gym, but I just don't have the time for it!"

It sends you screaming for the door to load up your motorcycle, find your next great adventure, ride off into the sunset...which only guarantees you'll be further removed when the next Christmas party rolls around.

Around this time you will run into the fifth stage of attrition – age. Or more specifically, the lack of energy.

Thankfully, some of your friends' children will be old enough to go to school and perhaps watch over themselves. They are no longer infants and a slight resurgence will occur where your buddies are happy to get out of the house, grab a beer, and get a little bit of "them time." It is also about this time you'll pick up some stragglers that will come from the wave of divorcees that is guaranteed to come. They'll be desperate to find a surrogate family as divorce destroyed theirs.

But while this might seem to be the renewal of a social life, the comeback of the "good ole gang" it isn't. And the reason why is because of age. They're just too tired.

After 40 years of life, 10 years of marriage, eight of them with children, and maybe a debilitating divorce or two thrown in there, your young and spry colleagues aren't so young or spry any more. They can't go for that weekly century bike ride you used to back in your college days, and they certainly don't have the time or money to go hiking in Rocky Mountain National Park. No, they have time for one beer and then...

"My gosh, it's 730PM! I better get home and get some sleep."

While you were staying in shape, working out, getting a doctorate, starting a company, learning welding, writing a novel, and pursuing life the vast majority of your friends were likely doing what everybody else did. Raising families, going into debt, working beleaguering jobs, raising children, getting divorced, and plain don't have the energy (or money) anymore for an effective social life. If anything it sends a false flag as you try to raise them to grab dinner, go for a run, perhaps get a drink, but they're having none of it. They're a shell of their former selves and are no longer capable of being part of an effective social life. After pulling enough teeth you slowly start to accept they are no longer your friends, but "people you used to know and occasionally see." And so you set out to form a new social life.

The sixth stage is the hunt. After trying to rally what remnants of your social circles remained with the success of Napoleon invading Russia, you go out into the world and try to make new friends. This is certainly possible, especially with the advent of the internet and social media such as Meet Up and Facebook, but here again statistics thwart the abnormally intelligent.

Nearly everybody has gone to some kind of co-ed sports program, joined a volleyball or kickball league, hoped to go out for beers afterwards, only to endure the same conversations about "Jimmy reading at an 8th grade level," swingystick, or sportzball. Nearly everybody goes to some kind of "wine and cheese show" where the local lousy art museum or theater holds a meet n' greet for "professionals." Again, conversation about "finishing my masters" and "did you see the latest TV cop-doctor-hospital-firefighter show" are abound. But attending these simply doesn't work because they are artificial, fabricated, short-lived, and do nothing to screen out average or dumb people. It's not until you look at some statistics and figures do you really see the challenge abnormally intelligent people face in simply making new friends. And Meet Up provides an amazing insight to this challenge.

The Twin Cities metro area holds a population of about 2.5 million. You would think with this population and the power of the internet you should be able to meet some like-minded individuals in adequate enough numbers you could reconstitute a new and vibrant social life. And so off I went, spending hours looking at the various and multiple types of groups out there.

I enjoy running so I joined the largest running group which boasts around 3,000 members. And after a couple runs I realized never more than 10 (usually around four) people show up for each run. Already you have a participation rate below 1% in one of the most successful Meet Up groups in the Twin Cities, and this was RUNNING. Not chess or "the nuclear physics enthusiasts" Meet Up.

Running however is not terribly cerebral and while I have indeed met some very nice people, none of us talked about the Federal Reserve's quantitative easing strategy, the latest problems in the Middle East, or the Scipio's tactics against Hannibal in the battle for Hispania. Looking for more mental stimulation I started looking for more specialized groups.

Masterminds has over 350 members.
Their last meeting was nine months ago.
Three whole people of which attended.

The Ayn Rand group has 27.
Their last meeting was also nine months ago.
And on average they get two people to attend each meeting.

Perhaps it was Minneapolis. Maybe the population is not large enough. So I looked at Chicago.

Their economics group meets quarterly.
Their last meeting was a quarter ago.
Six people, in a population of 8 million attended.
And this assumes I wanted to drive to Chicago.

About the most successful meeting I could find was the Twin Cities Austrian Economics Meet Up.

They have 300 members.
They do hold regular meetings.
Of which only seven attend regularly.

The larger point is to simply look at the numbers.
Even in major metro areas where the populations are in the *multiple of millions*, you can only get a *handful*

of people interested, and even then *only a fraction of them* show up. Yes, it is certainly possible you could make your greatest group of friends in those seven people who attend every month. And no, you don't need an entourage of 40 people to have a rewarding social life. But even with millions of people and the power of the internet to sift through them, it's still very hard for an abnormally intelligent person to simply "rebuild" a social life that rivals the one they had back in school.

It is here most high IQ people will have to resign themselves to the fact that no matter what they do, their previous social life, their original "proto-family" is not only never coming back, but will never be reconstituted. This doesn't mean you won't have friends. This doesn't mean you won't have a social life. It just won't be the intellectually-rewarding epicenter of your life like it was for the first third of your life. The sad truth is that environment won't return until you're either in a retirement community, assisted living, or (worse) a nursing home where the same elements of school are once again forced upon you.

There is, however, some good news.

While Chicago's population may only yield eight whole candidates for friendship, and the Twin Cities six, if you take the cumulative population of the country, even the world, there are in fact hundreds, even thousands of people who will and do make great friends. The problem is that they're spread across the globe, so how do you meet them, let alone have a social life with them?

Simple, the internet.

While the entire history of friendship implied physically meeting the person, this is no longer the case with the internet and social media such as Facebook. No doubt, you, me, and nearly anybody alive in the past 10 years has started to develop an active, vibrant, even close social network online, most of which are people we have never physically met. While this isn't ideal, it is a godsend because imagine what truly intelligent people did in the 1800's when they were condemned to live their entire lives in their local village and the people therein?

Today I have friends in Las Vegas, Switzerland, France, Lancaster, Charlotte, Atlanta, Morocco, Phoenix, San Diego, Dallas, Houston, Seattle, Chicago, Cincinnati, Calgary, Alaska, Regina, Toronto, Milan, London, Sydney, Melbourne, Perth, Singapore, India, Denver,

Sundance, Fargo, Berlin, Constantinople, Miami, Orlando, Mobile, New Orleans, and scores of places more.

Additionally, these are AMAZING and TRULY brilliant people.

And I don't mean that in a *"28 year old female writer for 'The New Yorker' bragging about her 'amazing' and 'gorgeous' friends. OMG, why can't they find a man, where's the red wine"* sort of way.

I mean that in the most literal sense of the words. They *are* AMAZING people who are BRILLIANT.

A pilot economist who is also part of his country's reserve military force.
A high end network security expert at the IMF.
A musician who is flown around the world to perform for millions.
A crazy window-washing Mexican philosopher who collects smoking pipes.
A retired officer who is an excellent gunsmith and master charcutier.
A statistics professor (and semi-pro gambler) who consults Vegas casinos about the profitability of different games...not to mention lets my girlfriend play with $1,000 chips at the blackjack table.

I could go on, but I would never have met this many people of such high quality and caliber had it not been for the internet. My intellectual and social life would be a fraction of what it is had I not the honor to meet these people online (and some, luckily, in person).

Of course digital friendships are not a perfect substitute for real-world friendships, but it is more intellectual stimulation than has ever been available to humans before. Yes, you're likely never to meet them all, and unfortunately you can't call them up to discuss politics at the local bar, but you are able to have conversations that would never have been possible just 30 years ago. Such great conversations between such great minds that it makes up for the fact your old analog social life no longer exists.

Dating

If maintaining a social life was an unwinnable battle, the world of dating is a veritable mine field for the abnormally intelligent. For whereas dealing with society in terms of attending school, going to college, going to work, and socializing was hard enough, dating introduces two new variables that make it particularly painful - hormones and emotion, specifically love.

These two variables make an already difficult situation nearly unbearable because it exploits our hard-wired biology and genetic programming to be loved by and have sex with the opposite sex. It's unbearable because we simply have no option. It is hard-wired. A man does not wake up one day and "decide" he no longer likes girls with long blond hair, big boobs, tight asses, and long legs. Just as women do not wake up and decide they don't like tall men, with dark features, lots of money, and a Hugh Jackmanesque-charm about them. We are genetically compelled to be sexually and emotionally attracted to the people we are regardless of our intelligence or our conscious intellectual desire not to be.

This genetic compulsion not only gets us in trouble, but causes great torment by attaching an unrequested sexual and emotional cost to our desires. It also commonly runs contrary to our best interests, taking a toll on our mental health, our finances, our love lives, nearly everything despite our "incredibly high IQ's." Sadly, it isn't until we've endured enough empirical hell do our frontal lobes start over-riding our smaller brains below and we start making wise decisions. But as always, we can't "solve biology." We can't simply "flip a switch" to make rational, reasoned decisions, ignoring what our hearts or loins desire. Ergo, the best we can do is acknowledge it, understand it, and caution against it, granting us the only solution to an unsolvable problem – sanity.

Dating for Abnormally Intelligent Men

Abnormally intelligent men face two unique and special problems when it comes to dating.

1. Very few equally-intelligent women to choose from
2. Not caring because their hormones are rendering their massive IQ's completely useless

The first problem is nothing new and to be expected. It is just a fact of statistics that if you're in the top 1% of intelligent men it's going to be a 1 in 100 chance of meeting an equally intelligent woman. However, whereas intelligent men could easily solve this problem if they used their brains, they instead choose to toss their brains into the garbage because "boobies!"

They could put a man on the moon.
Discover electricity.
Cure scores of diseases.

Build supercomputers.

But you throw a cute girl into the mix, and they couldn't solve 2+2. Their smaller head has simply overrode the larger one.

For this they pay an egregious and inordinate price. And the reason why is the "Hot Crazy Matrix."

The "Hot Crazy Matrix" is the creation of Dana McLendon, a lawyer from Tennessee. The basic tenet of the theory is that the hotter a girl is the more likely she is to be crazy. The only problem is this isn't a theory. It's 100% true.

The hotter a girl the more she is shielded from the realities of life because

1. Men want to have sex with her and
2. Women want to be her

Ergo, she is given all sorts of advantages in life that her less-attractive peers aren't. She gets more job offers, higher paying jobs, more dates paid for, more sugar daddies, easier terms of credit, more favorable contracts, less punishment, less discipline, and the list goes on. In the end you do not have a hardened, empirically driven adult, but a spoiled adult-child that is accustomed to getting what she wants for (more or less) free. And if she doesn't get what she wants, she'll usually throw some kind of tantrum as it has gotten her what she wanted in the past. Regardless, the point is the more beautiful the woman, the less likely she is to be a stable, sane, self-supporting adult.

This presents a paradox then to all red-blooded men in the world. Their entire genetic programming, over two million years of evolution is SCREAMING at the man to, at all costs, date, court, and inevitably impregnate the girl with the ample bosom, long legs, an hour glass figure, and a bi-polar disorder. But unless the man is Hugh Jackman or George Clooney, the woman has been conditioned by society to be insufferable. She has also been conditioned to extract as much time, financial, emotional, and psychological resources out of that man. And thus the situation we are all familiar with (perhaps experienced ourselves) – a man who is, infatuated with a woman that is out of his league, who is also a controlling manipulative psychopath that treats him like utter crap, the abuse of which is only temporarily placated upon the receipt of gifts, money, or resources.

I would like to say,

"It takes a bit, but after dating three or four of these emotional, psychological vampires men inevitably wise up around the age of 30,"

but many, if not, most don't. Matter of fact, men with high IQ's usually get the worst of it in that they're inexperienced and therefore easy marks for gold-diggers who have financial troubles in the form of another man's child, student loans, or some other consequence of Idiocracy. It isn't until an intervention occurs or the man suffers enough does he make the conscious effort to start making decisions with his larger head and not his small one. And instead of insisting on "just pretty," he settles for "smart and pretty enough."

Still, this does not undo the nearly-guaranteed two decades of hell all men (both smart and dumb) will suffer from puberty till about 30. In forfeiting their intelligence AND preferring to chase beauty over intelligence, men condemn themselves to suffering the traits of stupid, but pretty girls.

Being stood up
Paying for dates that lead nowhere
Brain damage caused from painfully stupid conversation
Flake outs

Credit card debt
Student loans
Worthless degrees
"But I have a boyfriend in Madagascar"
"My girlfriend just broke up with her boyfriend and needs me now."
"If you can't handle me at my worst, then you definitely don't deserve me at my best"
"I just can't hold a job."
"I want to be an actress."
Opinions on what Orpah said
Reality TV
Friend-zoning
And a potpourri of other assorted painassery associated with dating dumb, but pretty girls.

Ergo, if a man at any age, can wake up, understand the "Hot Crazy Matrix," make the conscious decision to have standards, and insist on intelligent, accomplished, sane women they can turn their dating lives from a hellish experience to one that is "about as good as it will ever get."

It all depends, however, on overriding the little brain with the big one. And that is an intellectual challenge larger than solving cold fusion.

Dating for Abnormally Intelligent Women

Intelligent women face the same fundamental problem intelligent men do when it comes to dating - there just aren't that many smart men to go around. And like men, intelligent women have to kiss a lot of frogs to find their intellectual-equivalent prince. But whereas men's additional dating problems primarily stem from their small head leading the larger one around, abnormally intelligent women's dating problems hail from a conflict between biology and modern day social norms.

While the push for women's equality has been successful in how women are treated in terms of law, suffrage, work, education, etc., the problem is merely having different laws for the past 100 or so years does not change the biology that has been at work for 2 million. And whether it's politically correct to say so or not, humans (and most species) have evolved where the man is the predominant partner in the relationship and women the subservient ones. This has not only been engrained in our psychologies for the past 2 million years, but the structure of our society since recorded history.

This presents abnormally intelligent women with a common problem. While they may very well indeed be more intelligent than the man they're dating, it does not undo the genetic and social conditioning both men and women have. This creates a conflict wherein the woman is smarter, and could very well be the better decision maker, but since the man has traditionally been the leader in human relationships her superior intelligence causes unintentional friction. This manifests itself in various ways. Some men get angry, as they subconsciously fear their biological role being usurped, but are unable to explain why they're right and why the woman is wrong. Others dismiss what the more-intelligent woman is saying as simply "being a woman," continuing on the wrong path of whatever the disagreement may be. Worse, some men become abusive, convincing otherwise intelligent women they're stupid, very much like a 2.1 GPA fools a genius child into thinking they're dumb. Of course, a lot of this is not conscious (bar the blatantly abusive boyfriend), but rather instinctual where millions of years of evolution in the man is rejecting a woman as the leader or a superior. But while this may explain the phenomenon, it still causes strife for abnormally intelligent women while dating.

Closely related to the engrained genetic programming "men must lead," it is not uncommon for smarter women to constantly be challenged to some meaningless competition by their less-intelligent partners. Much like a smart person at a party will endure the "one-upmanship" of a jealous party-goer, a less-intelligent man may compensate by finding some realm they are superior in compared to their girlfriend. Sports, meaningless trivia, their "fratboy days," anything that will give them the edge, no matter how frivolous or pointless it is. The girlfriend has no desire to compete, and certainly does not disrespect her boyfriend, but the genetic compunction to be "superior" in at least something gnaws at some men's psyches until they unnecessarily challenge their girlfriends in something that truly doesn't matter. Again, this does nothing but create headaches for abnormally intelligent women.

Also related to genetically-enforced traditional roles is many high IQ women, even though smarter, still want the man to take the lead. Be it ballroom dancing, approaching them to ask them on a date, or throwing themselves into a pack of hungry saber-tooth tigers, women, in general, prefer men to lead. This can be difficult, however, if it's obvious the woman is smarter. Her intelligence may intimidate the man into a follower role. Her intelligence may have her accidentally and unconsciously slide into the role of leader. Or the man may be smart enough to say, *"Wait! Why should I lead!? You're the smarter one between us! I'm an idiot! You should be in charge!"*

wisely abdicating his role. This may be the "smart" thing to do, but it's not what many woman viscerally desire in their hearts.

Then there's boredom.

Men, for whatever natural gifts they have usually can put on a good show and put their best foot forward. They are after all the aggressors and usually have developed some ability to be charming and clever by which to woo women. An abnormally intelligent woman may be tickled by his fancies, leading her to believe he truly is intelligent, when in reality it's just a rehearsed and fleeting act. After dating a bit he simply can't keep up the charming charade and the woman quickly finds out how intelligent (or not) he really is. This is often where you'll see a girl all giddy upon meeting a "new guy" only to find out a month later he was "a jerk." Still abnormally intelligent women are not so much let down that he's a jerk, as much as they are that his intellect could not captivate them long term.

Finally, the most common complaint I hear from my female clients under 40 is the lack of real, masculine men. While pursuing the ideal of equal treatment of the sexes, various faux-intellectuals and hacks posing as "social scientists" have pushed beyond equal treatment under the law and now demand equal outcomes and equal...well...everything.

Anything men can do, women can do.
Applauding Bruce/Catlyn Jenner more than young girls majoring in engineering.
Besmirching women for daring to want to be wives and moms.
"Gender is a social construct."
Replacing "he" and "she" with "zhe" and "zhr."
As well as the complete elimination of gender entirely.

This perilously ignores the terabytes of empirical data (not to mention fact) that men and women are different and that these differences cannot be erased no matter how hard you try. It also ignores the obvious point that these differences exist for some pretty damn good reasons and likely shouldn't be trifled with.

Men have penises, women have vaginas. They are designed that way to breed children. Women have breasts, produce milk, and are more nurturing. They are designed that way to take care of and nurture children. Men have testosterone, are bigger, stronger, faster and (by some measures) smarter than women. They are designed that way to provide for and protect their families. And forget the obvious physiological differences. Just look at the history of how men, women, and society have *naturally* organized themselves over the millennia across different cultures. I find it very cute and adorable "social scientists" of the past 50 years think they know more than what nature has figured out over the past 2 million.

Still, the academic and political classes of society thought it best to trifle with these realities, blurring the lines of gender, which has ultimately resulted in pansified, emasculated men that no woman wants. Yes, television says women want "sensitive 90's men." Yes, academia says men need to get in touch with their "emotions and inner-selves." And yes, even women say they want that bearded hipster with his red skinny jeans who writes poetry, works at the coffee shop, lives at home, and can't afford a car.

But it's almost as cute as "social scientists" thinking they know more than nature.

No matter what society, politicians, media, even women themselves say, their genes want a tall, rugged, strong, brilliant, charming, clever, brute of a man who can rock her world in bed and crush the skulls of any interloper who threatens her children.

Unfortunately, these social experiments with gender are doubly damaging to the dating lives of abnormally intelligent women. For while it's already difficult enough to find equally intelligent men to date, which men precisely do you think are most likely to succumb to society's push to eliminate masculinity and tell men to be more feminine? It certainly isn't going to be Brock the Jock who's been getting laid since he could throw a football the furthest in the 8th grade. And it's not going to be Stoner Joe who could supply the female dregs in high school with pot who's getting laid. It's going to be the cerebral, "smart" boys who did what their elders told them. It's going to be the highly intelligent who are most trusting and, therefore, prone to swallow whole the "sensitive 90's man" tripe being pushed down their throats. Alas, instead of pursuing intelligence AND masculinity (which is a deadly combination that slays the ladies) they pursue intelligence, emotion, feelings, and femininity at the EXPENSE of masculinity.

Leaving nothing but emasculated nerds who may stimulate a women's intellect, but do nothing to drop her panties.

Marriage

Biological urges don't end at dating because invariably they are driving people towards two larger goals:

1. Children
2. Pair-bonding

The statistical unlikelihood of smart people breeding considered, not to mention birth control making the debate about children moot, it doesn't change the strong biological urge you have to go and at least participate in the act of sex. So while you may or may not want children, your Neanderthal brain still screams at your frontal lobes to go through the motions anyway...and won't stop yelling until you do.

Likewise, because of 2 million years of genetic programming and breeding, your Neanderthal brain is also screaming at your frontal lobes to find one person to pair-bond with. This not only increased the chances of survival for your offspring, but also has served as a source for companionship, love, support, and other sources of endorphins for humans over the genetic millennia.

When you take these two huge biological forces and combine them with the guaranteed hell abnormally intelligent people suffer when dating, unless you're a particularly savvy player or particularly good looking woman, you'll be screaming to find the love of your life, settle down, and get married.

Still, as it always does, statistics flummox abnormally intelligent people's love life. However, this time not in the traditional sense where there's merely a shortage of smart people to go around, but rather it is statistics about the abnormally intelligent themselves that trips them up. Specifically, intelligence is NOT distributed equally among men and women. The bell distribution of intelligence for men and women do NOT match and therefore causes an imbalance. And as you would guess, this imbalance disproportionately affects the abnormally intelligent.

Depending on the source, men and women either have the exact same average IQ OR men are slightly more intelligent (with a mean score of about 3 points higher). Regardless, while the average is roughly the same the bell distribution of intelligence between men and women is not. Women have a much more tightly bounded curve while men's intelligence curve is flatter. What this means is for all intents and purposes men and women average out to about the same IQ, but there are more intelligent men than women AND more stupid men than women. In other words, most NASA employees are men, just as most homeless people are men, but we all average out to be the same.

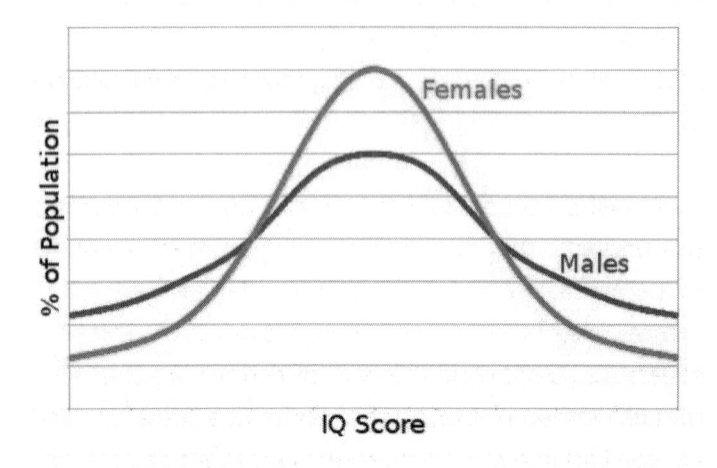

[Figure: Bell curve distributions of IQ Score (x-axis) vs % of Population (y-axis), showing a taller, narrower curve labeled "Females" and a shorter, wider curve labeled "Males".]

This creates some interesting imbalances on both sides of the bell distribution curve. First, at about one standard deviation above average there are approximately the same number of men and women at this IQ level. In short, if you have an IQ of 115 there are about the same number of women/men out there for you to date. This would be ideal in that this market is in "equilibrium" and every one should find themselves a similarly intelligent spouse. But if you go much further past an IQ of 115, the number of women rapidly drops relative to the number of men. So quickly that by the time you reach two standard deviations above average *there are two men for every one woman. (The statistics vary significantly based on the studies you're citing and their methodologies. However, if you wanted to further research this topic a good place to start is here: http://www.iqcomparisonsite.com/sexdifferences.aspx)*

The most obvious implication is the huge drawback this presents for abnormally intelligent men. At an IQ of 130 most abnormally intelligent men are in a market for a wife where the buyers outnumber the sellers 2:1. Following the laws of economics this means women this intelligent come at a premium and we see this in every engineering class there ever was. There's always that one girl surrounded by 18 guys, all vying to be her lab partner, help her with homework (sometimes DO HER HOMEWORK), bring her flowers, or whatever it was that engineering students did to woo those girls.

Unfortunately, there's only so many "hot IT chicks" to go around and these women are picked off rather quickly, forcing most abnormally intelligent men to date dumber. Of course you can certainly date within +/- 10 IQ points of your own intelligence and not have it be a huge romantic obstacle, but in order for this market to balance, SOME men have to go to the other side of 115 where there's a surplus of women. And this can make for some tedious, often painful relationships. Still, it is what it is, and is just another drawback of "The Curse of the High IQ."

But while abnormally intelligent women may think this is cause for celebration, think again. At first it may be great to be the center of attention in Calc I, but by Calc III all that male attention gets tiresome, even obtrusive. You can't just "go to class and get your degree in engineering." You can't just "be an engineer at Honeywell." An entire unwanted micro-celebrity status is conferred upon you where you're constantly asked out, constantly approached by cowardly nerds too afraid to ask you out, not to mention the stalkers who view you as their personal property and have issues with boundaries.

Economic problems of imbalanced marriage markets aside, there is one final problem that both high IQ men and women face when it comes to marriage. And that is how progressive credentialism undermines abnormally intelligent people's ability to get married and have kids.

Again it is laughable that it takes 20 years of schooling and education to "finally" be considered employable by today's employers. The truth is if we got rid of all the fat, all the unnecessary pre-requisite classes, and allowed students to advance as fast as their intelligence allowed them, we would be graduating engineers and doctors at 18, 19, 20, and 21. Additionally, if we cared anything about the children and their futures, we would make it so they would not be indebted to the tune of $250,000 in student or med school loans. This would not only accelerate their careers, saving a full decade of their lives, but provide for much sounder finances making marriage and starting a family a viable option for young people (much as it was in the 1940's).

But, as we know, the various powers that be need their pound of flesh and so we perpetually increase the qualifications and credentials one needs to land a job, let alone one that pays enough to support a family. And so it's not until we're darn well near 30 are we even remotely capable of thinking about marriage and children.

But abnormally intelligent people face another quandary. While they have to go through school like everybody else, since they tend to study real subjects that are infinitely more difficult than the "social sciences," "humanities," and "liberal arts," it isn't until they're graduating from med school, dental school, or finishing their actuarial certifications can they even get employed. And forget employed, there's at least five years of debts to pay off. In short, abnormally intelligent people can expect to be well into their mid 30's, perhaps even early 40's before they are financially stable enough to consider marriage. This presents a different set of problems for both high IQ men and women.

When it comes to men they get off relatively easy here. Men's sperm does not have an expiration date on it and they can, in theory, start families until the day they die. Of course, they may not have the same number of intelligent women in their age group to choose from, but this may also be why they tend to date younger. Not only are most of those highly intelligent women spoken for, many of them are approaching the age they can no longer bear children. In this sense men trade intelligence in for beauty and youth (which we of course know "NEVER" happens in the real world), but with that comes the increased chance of divorce and painful conversations with a younger, less-intelligent spouse.

Women, however, face a VERY daunting prospect when it comes to progressive credentialism crowding out marriage. Since it took them effectively 30 years of their youth to get qualified in an advanced, high IQ field, their youth and beauty is unfortunately gone and with it, their primary bargaining chip to lasso a man into marriage. What's worse is that when you combine the already statistically low chances of meeting equally intelligent men (in the general population) and that those few men are likely emasculated and physically unattractive, it is very possible you won't meet a man you're compatible with until you can no longer safely bear children.

This sadly leads to a problem we're already familiar with and that is the fact the stupid people are breeding and the intelligent are not. Not only does this promise the ramifications of Idiocracy for society and the future of the human race, it also deprives the highly intelligent of families and any joy they might have derived from them. Because of progressive credentialism, the education system, and the fact higher-intellectual fields require more time to master them, abnormally intelligent people may simply be too old to pass on their genes to the future, let alone leave a legacy for themselves.

Thankfully the future is practically guaranteed to be an Idiocracy.

CHAPTER 6
PSYCHOLOGY

Mental Illness

Vincent Van Gogh, Alan Turing, Ernest Hemmingway, George Eastman, and Hunter S. Thompson, just to name a few, are the stereotypically archetypes of the "tortured genius." Driven to suicide or madness (or both) they could no longer tolerate society and actually preferred to end their lives than endure what was presumably another painful day of life. Were they so bored by society there was nothing left for them to live for? Was society incapable of providing them with intellectual peers? Or perhaps did they have genuine mental diseases that, geniuses or not, would have led to suicide anyway? Regardless of the reason, it does highlight another drawback of being abnormally intelligent – mental illness.

It's no secret that mental illness runs rife amongst the abnormally intelligent. We all know they commit suicide at higher rates. We all know they are more depressed than their dumber counterparts. We all know they drink more alcohol and do more drugs. And we all know their intelligence is so alienatingly-high they can actually be "lonely in a crowd."

Or do we?

For while it's assumed that intelligent people typically have more mental problems, drink more, and are more likely to commit suicide, the truth is...

we don't know.

The most shocking thing discovered while researching this topic is just how little research has been conducted on intelligence versus things like mental illness, drug abuse, depression, suicide, etc., yet nearly everybody is *absolutely convinced* abnormally intelligent people suffer these psychological afflictions. What's also shocking is what research has been done in this field is incredibly flimsy providing neither proof nor disproof of a relationship between mental health and IQ. And when the entirety of the research is compiled and considered the best we can conclude is somewhere between "maybe" and "likely."

First, there is some concrete evidence that intelligence is associated with some mental disorders, specifically depression, bipolar disorder, schizophrenia and others. However, this evidence comes from two dozen-plus studies done within the past 10 years and are really more the first exploratory studies into the subject of intelligence and mental illness. In other words, they can't be considered 100% conclusive, but their data indicates a high likelihood there is at least *some* correlation between mental illness and intelligence.

Then there are scores of articles, "studies," and "research papers" written or cited by the media, but oddly lacking the original source. There are also opinion papers written by psychologists, neurologists, and other professionals, all of which "observe," "theorize," "opine," or "suggest" a relationship between IQ and mental disorders, but never prove. In short, people are observing this phenomenon in society to the point there's enough anecdotal evidence to write about it, but, again, it has yet to be proven.

Because of this, I decided to do my own research to see if a relationship between IQ and mental health could be sussed out. And so in a very linear and unemotional way I took the two simplest variables I could imagine that would measure intelligence and mental illness:

IQ and suicide rates by country.

Originally the results were conclusive. There is ABSOLUTELY NO correlation between the average IQ of a population and their suicide rate. The R-squared factor being .002.

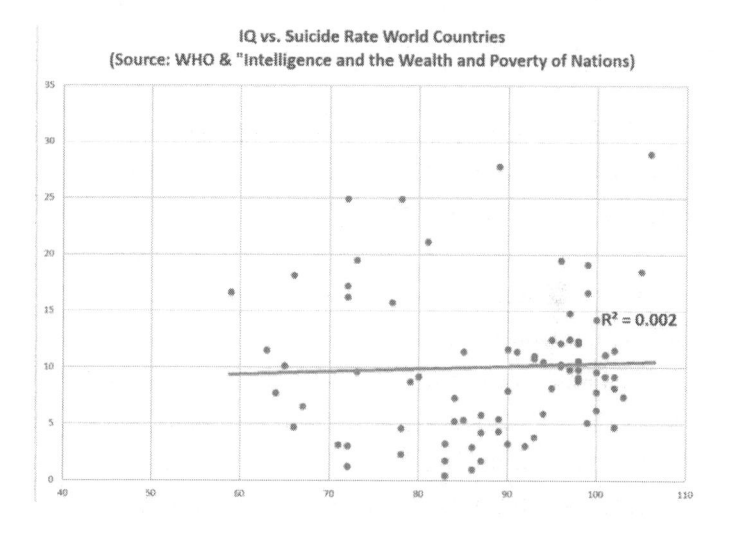

IQ vs. Suicide Rate World Countries
(Source: WHO & "Intelligence and the Wealth and Poverty of Nations)

$R^2 = 0.002$

However, this considered all countries in the world (where data was available, N=80) where dramatic differences in culture and other variables would confound the data. When we focus on first world countries only (where things like "depression" and "bipolar" are our main problems and not "clean water," "food," and "not getting killed by the local warlord") there is a slight positive relationship between IQ and suicide in these homogenized countries. An R-square factor of .11.

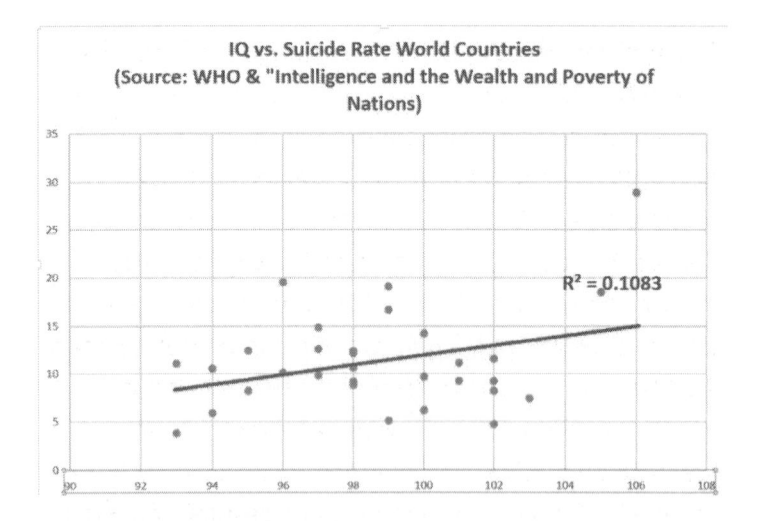

IQ vs. Suicide Rate World Countries
(Source: WHO & "Intelligence and the Wealth and Poverty of Nations)

$R^2 = 0.1083$

Still, as stated before this is not proof, but falls again within the domain of "pointing to" or "suggesting" there is a relationship between intelligence and mental disorders.

So in conclusion, there is none. There "might" be a relationship between intelligence and mental illness. Smart people "might" have more psychological issues than dumber ones. But the data does not prove it so it must not exist.

There's just one problem.

Tell that to abnormally intelligent people who are indeed suffering mentally.

The problem with the research done thus far in the psychological/mental illness profession is that there really is none. As mentioned before it is SHOCKING how little research has been done on this topic. Therefore, the ABSENCE of research does not mean "proof the relationship between intelligence and mental illness doesn't exist." It means more research needs to be done before anything can be determined. Additionally, the social sciences, psychology most prominent among them, does not exactly have a stellar record when it comes to the integrity of their research. A recent study found the results of 2/3rds of psychological studies could not be repeated, calling into question the entirety of the profession.

This forces us to do something that humans have been relying upon for the past 2 million years, and that is trust our eyes. With no conclusive proof one way or the other, not to mention the social "sciences" aren't terribly trustworthy, one merely has to look at their intelligent friends and see if they are suffering some kind of psychological problem. And if you do, you will likely find that not only do most of them suffer mentally in one capacity or another, but the most pressing problem they have in life is some sort of depression, mania, regret, boredom, or ennui that is just keeping them down. And it is here we need a more practical and functional theory as to the origin and causes of these problems if we ever hope to solve them.

An Alternative Theory

While researchers and psychologists pussyfoot about and maybe get around to researching this topic further, the answer to the abnormally intelligent's mental problems may lie in Maslow's Hierarchy of Needs.

Maslow's Hierarchy of Needs basically states that in order to advance as a human there is an order in which you do it. Certain needs cannot be satisfied until those under it are taken care of, thus a "hierarchy of needs." So you can't be pursuing your doctorate in finance if you don't have food on the table, just as you can't think about asking Suzy Q on a date if your position is about to be overrun by Al-Qaeda terrorists.

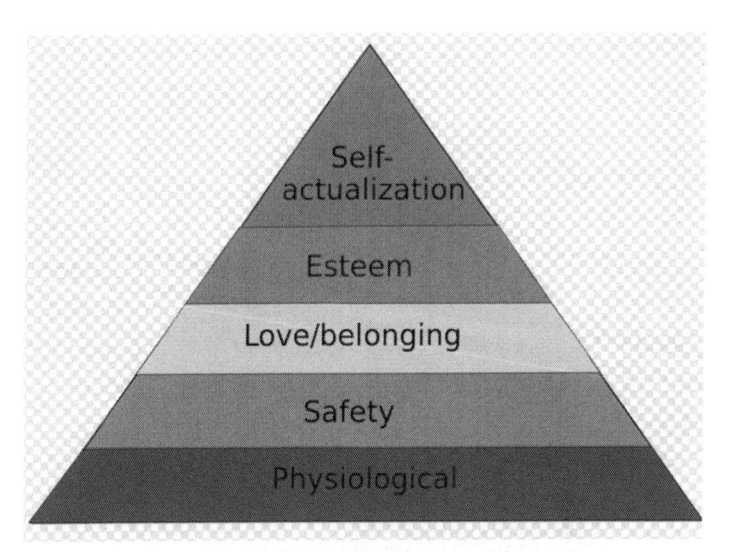

Image by FireFlySixtySeven

However, whereas Maslow's Hierarchy of Needs primarily focuses on advancement and self-improvement, it can also be viewed in terms of the severity of problems you face in life. And it is through this lens we can start to understand the problems facing abnormally intelligent people.

To be bluntly honest, "mental illness" really is a "First World Problem." They don't have things such as "bipolar" or "social anxiety disorder" or "affluenza" in Pakistan. Your average Ecuadorian does not refer to the village psychologist as "her psychologist" like an American soccer mom who has "her psychologist" on speed dial. And the average kid in Turkey does not suffer from "ADD" or "ADHD." They have infinitely more pressing matters such as poverty, terrorism, death, and disease on their minds.

This isn't to belittle the mental problems people suffer (first world or not), but it is to highlight where people focus the majority of their mental faculties depending on where they are in the hierarchy. It is also to point out that the biggest problems people face in their life is determined by where they are in Maslow's Hierarchy, not how their problems rank in the world.

For example consider two men.

There is a soldier whose wife just sent him a "Dear John" letter, telling him she's divorcing him and taking the kids. He has also been informed by the bank that his mortgage has not been paid and is going to be foreclosed upon. He can't do anything as he's in Iraq and on patrol, when suddenly he is captured by ISIS.

The second man is a retired surgeon. He ran a successful practice for 40 years, has $20 million in the bank, saved many lives, and through hard work has afforded himself every luxury life could offer. He has visited every country he ever wanted, done everything he's ever wanted to do, ate everything he wanted to eat, and now sits there at his Floridian mansion depressed because there really is nothing left to do. His friends are all dead or living in other parts of the country. His wife passed away. And he awkwardly tries to spark conversation with the landscapers who come in weekly to tend his estate, too embarrassed to ask if they'd like to get a beer.

Who has it worse?

Obviously, the poor solider captured by ISIS does. He could die at any moment, and certainly be tortured along the way.

But whose problem is solvable?

Soon, a SEAL team bursts in, takes out all the ISIS members and rescues the poor soldier. Meanwhile, back in Florida the doctor tries to invite the landscaper to a beer, but he doesn't speak English, so the doctor goes back to pour himself another scotch to avoid his loneliness.

But the real question is who's happier?

The poor soldier, despite having horrendous problems at home and still being WAY below the doctor on Maslow's Hierarchy of Needs is ECSTATIC because the immediate problem he was facing (survival) was solved. He's not going to die. He won't be tortured. He can now move on to solve whatever problems he faces at home.

The doctor, despite having all the luxuries the world can afford is alone, has no mental stimulation, and is depressed. The problem he faces is there are no problems to face anymore, and because of the ennui he pulls out a gun and kills himself.

This sad and tragic example highlights two things.

One, happiness is relative and dependent upon solving your problems at your particular level in Maslow's Hierarchy of Needs. To be able to progress, giving you some sense of control over your destiny and that it is going the right way.

Two, people can progress to the point there are no problems, they literally can be living the dream. But while technology, innovation, and free markets have advanced to the point some people literally have no problems, our biology and genetics have not. We've been genetically programmed for 2 million years to solve problems and advance. And it is so rare in the entirety of the human experience not to have problems that our brains simply don't know how to deal with it. In the words of Agent Smith from "Matrix,"

"Did you know that the first Matrix was designed to be a perfect human world? Where none suffered, where everyone would be happy. It was a disaster. No one would accept the program. Entire crops were lost. Some believed we lacked the programming language to describe your perfect world. But I believe that, as a species, human beings define their reality through suffering and misery. The perfect world was a dream that your primitive cerebrum kept trying to wake up from."

And it is this second aspect that (I contend) is the cause of the majority of mental problems high IQ people face today.

IQ is one of the most reliable indicators of future success. Financial, educational, professional, familial, and social. There may be some bumps along the road, but in the long run smarter people more quickly assess reality, bending it to their will, capitalizing on it, improving and advancing their lives. However, many, if not most abnormally intelligent people will reach the point where there are no problems or very few in their lives. This lack of problems results in a lack of purpose and agency as it strikes at the core of our genetic programming that makes us feel as if we are worthless since we have no problems to solve. You combine this with the statistical rarity of equally intelligent peers and you are completely in a world of your own, metaphorically alone, with nothing to do, and no problems to solve.

Boredom sets in.
Loneliness is forced upon you.
Perhaps there's even a brush with nihilism.
And unlike being an ISIS hostage, there is no solution because there is no problem.

Drugs and Alcohol

"I drink because I'm bored."
      -Bill Burr

Bill Burr is one of the funniest and most prominent comedians in the world today. He started his career in the early 90's from scratch. He had no tutors, no coaches, no mentors, and just started writing his own material, hitting up no-name comedy clubs in strip malls because he had a determination for work and a passion for comedy. Inexorably Bill refined his acts, developed new and improved material, polished his presentation, and after 20 years of hard and grueling work became one of the funniest men alive.

Today, Bill is no longer the "dental assistant" he once was working under his father. He has performed at Carnegie Hall, Madison Square Garden multiple times, has multiple comedy specials, has done several "other-continent" tours, flown around the world, and has had a handful of roles in various movies and TV shows. If that wasn't enough, he hosts a twice-weekly podcast (The Monday Morning Podcast), is a cigar aficionado, works out regularly, is married to The Lovely Nia, has a dog, is an avid drummer (sitting in one time with Slash from Guns and Roses), is a helicopter pilot, and oh, that's right, produced his own cartoon, "F is for Family."

There's just one question.

How in hell's name is Bill Burr bored?

The answer is sadly simple.

Because the man is a genius and there's nothing in this world that will satiate his intellect.

The problem in being abnormally intelligent is that you are likely to become successful. And once that happens you run into the paradox that your only problem is you ran out of problems. Worsening this situation is you likely strove immensely to get where you are and, assuming (like most successful people) it didn't happen overnight, but rather years, if not decades, that work ethic is part of your permanent psyche and cannot be changed or removed. In other words, not only do you have no problems to solve, you have a constant level of mania and energy that has nowhere to go.

Fortunately, there are three ways to solve this. Unfortunately, all of them are drugs.

The first and most socially-acceptable solution is alcohol. Bill Burr, despite everything he has done and is doing in his life, struggles with alcohol. Not because he's an "alcoholic," but as he admitted to before, *"I drink because I'm bored."* Of course, we ask how can this be when his life is the *complete antithesis of boring*, but again it's because no amount of activities, projects, or adventure will fully satiate his mind and intellect. Ergo, instead of trying to control the world around you, seeking out that magical intellectually-satiating hobby (that doesn't exist), you instead control how your mind interprets the world.

You get drunk.

Of course, Bill is not alone here because while IQ and mental illness are not conclusively linked, *ALCOHOL CONSUMPTION AND IQ MOST DEFINITELY ARE*. Any search on the internet will pull up scores of studies and piles of research that show, quite convincingly, there is a positive relationship between intelligence and alcohol consumption. And any visit to an AA meeting will introduce you to a minor-league MENSA club. But while academics and researchers may chalk the relationship between IQ and alcohol up to "a curiosity to experiment" most geniuses drink to simply turn off their minds. They realize nothing in the world will truly satiate them, nothing will give them agency and purpose again, so instead of beating their head against a problem with no solution, they numb it to the point of blissful indifference.

The second solution is just like alcohol, but illegal - drugs.

Like alcohol there is ample research showing high IQ people are likely to do more drugs. Again researchers suggest this has to do with curiosity, but also believe some of the correlation is driven by the price of illegal narcotics, which necessitates a higher income, and thus relates to higher IQ's. Regardless of these technical differences, drugs serve the exact same purpose in the lives of the abnormally intelligent people who use them. It is an escape from their otherwise unchallenging and uninteresting lives wherein it's easier to change their brain than the world around them. The only difference is the level of addiction, not to mention their illegality, which is why alcohol use is much higher than drug use.

Finally there is "sublimation." Sublimation is the psychological term used to describe taking any energy or impulses you have and ensuring you channel them towards good and productive purposes. For example, you may have gotten laid off from your job and while you desperately would like to murder your boss, you instead channel that anger into lifting weights at the gym. Or you can't fall asleep at night (another common problem of abnormally intelligent people) so you decide to write a book about abnormally intelligent people instead. Whatever the case, you take the excess energy you have, find something that interests you, and pursue it with reckless, but productive abandon. And here Bill Burr is another perfect example.

He flies helicopters, plays the drums, smokes cigars, works out, is learning how to cook, does his podcast, produces a cartoon, and *excels in all of them in a very short period of time*.

So you may be asking,

"Well what the heck is the drawback about sublimation? And how the heck is it a drug? Sounds like one of the best things you can do, actually."

And you're right. Sublimation is a very productive, if not "the" most productive way to expend all the extra energy you have. But it's still a drug. And the reason why is because you're using it like one.

Sublimation is nothing more than the pursuit of novelty. Your brain is bored, and so you seek some kind of new intellectual adventure. It can be a hobby, a trip, a skill, or a project, but what you are doing is no different than plying your brain with booze or drugs. You are simply distracting your mind from the fact that ultimately you're bored with life and really have no agency or purpose. But while sublimation may be the "best" drug out there, it still comes at a cost. Specifically, the loss of novelty.

Like building a tolerance to alcohol or drugs, you will also build up a tolerance to novelty. Worse, if you're particularly aggressive, you'll build up a tolerance very quickly. For example I started riding motorcycles in 2009. Four short years later I had taken motorcycle trips to Sturgis, Beartooth Pass, Monument Valley,

Banff, Jasper, and finally, Alaska. Upon returning from my Alaska trip, my motorcycle sat for about two weeks before I rode it again because I was plum sick of riding. I did more riding in a year than most avid cyclists did in a lifetime, and thus destroyed the "novelty" the drug of motorcycle riding gave me.

The solution may simply be "find another hobby," but often times it isn't. The abnormally intelligent, like a drug addict, needs a bigger hit so you have something to look forward to. This prompts you to become an adrenaline junkie. First it was sewing, then it was kayaking, then mountain climbing, then canyoneering, then skydiving, then hang-gliding, then shark-hunting, then shark-hunting-while-hang-gliding.

Admittedly, this may be a bit tongue-in-cheek, but it still highlights the fact you can never solve the problem that doesn't exist. You can only treat it. You can only numb your mind to it (as you destroy your liver and kidneys) with alcohol and drugs or run away from it with a never-ending list of hobbies and adventures. It won't be until you have truly intellectual minds in your life (be it your spouse, colleagues, or nearby friends) and in adequate numbers will your brain get the mental stimulation it needs. And since these precious few people are so rare, you might as well develop a taste for scotch, a passion for hiking, and an appreciation for Bill Burr's comedy.

CHAPTER 7
LIMITING GREATNESS

It is a given that for the vast majority of people the most important thing in their lives will be their families, their spouses, and their children. Following the axiom "humans are the most important thing in the world," family is typically followed closely by friends or other loved ones, perhaps extended families. But while these people may be the most precious things in our lives, in the grand scheme of humanity they are nothing unique in that nearly everybody has a family and next to breathing, breeding is the most common thing humans do.

This status quo has been completely satisfactory for the vast majority of humans throughout human history. Most people are perfectly happy in having a family, wasting two hours a day in a commute, eight hours a day in a cube, 25 years in school, seven years in a marriage, eight years in a second marriage, feeding their gullet, watching the game, drinking light beers, dying in a nursing home, making no notable or mentionable contributions to society their entire lives. And while this may sound a bit harsh and judgmental it's true, and much more than you realize.

List all the notable humans throughout recorded history that come to mind. Now, grab all the history books or the resources of the internet and come up with a list of every notable person ever recorded in history. Henry Ford, Julius Caesar, Erwin Rommel, Genghis Khan, Gilgamesh, Plato, large and small, you name it. If you're lucky you'll come up with 10,000 people, but let's be generous and say 100,000.

That 100,000 are the humans who have shaped and molded this world. The ones who are 100% responsible for all the successes and tragedies of all of humanity. They are the ones history will remember forever and the ones who will define this planet until it is consumed by the sun.

Now divide that by the 100 billion humans that are estimated to have lived since recorded history.

The number you should get is .000001. Or .0001%.

ONE TEN THOUSANDTH OF ONE PERCENT of the human population has achieved anything noteworthy in the history of the world. That means 99.9999% of the population hasn't, and have lived regular, ordinary lives that will be forever lost to obscurity, commonness, and mediocrity. There is no record of them, nor any trace of them, ultimately meaning their fleeting existence in this universe served no purpose and was wasted. It's as if they never lived in the first place. But we are alive here and now and have the raw intellectual capacity to not suffer such similar fates. Thus, we owe it to ourselves to follow the wise words of Cypress Hill,

"We aint' goin' out like that."

"We Ain't Goin' Out Like That"

This isn't to say that if you live a normal life with a family it would be wasted. Nor is it saying abnormally intelligent people demand fame or insist on going down in the history books. But high IQ people do have the intelligence to realize they are finite, they're going to die, and that this one life should not be wasted doing the same thing 99.9999% of the world's population did. We don't need statues erected in our honor. We don't need to win world wars and free hundreds of millions of people. And we don't need to cure a devastating disease. But we need to do something with our lives, our intellects, and our capacities beyond merely breeding.

This then gets to the most important thing in the life of an abnormally intelligent person - their legacy. What are they going to achieve with their life? What are they going to do that will ultimately define their flash-in-the-pan existence in the universe? Since everybody dies and you only get this ONE, PRECIOUS, SHORT, FINITE shot on this planet, the absolute worst thing a highly intelligent person can do with it is waste it being common. Ergo, most smart people in some capacity or another, at some level of another, wish to achieve greatness.

What form this greatness ultimately manifests itself in depends on the person. Some will start companies. Some will becoming engineers. One person may cure cancer. Another may become the world's greatest guitar player ever. But what they won't be is the everyday, average-intelligence schlub mindlessly going through their days, rapidly approaching death, wasting the only life they'll ever have. We simply insist on making our lives great.

But we all know where that type of thinking leads. And once you start acting on your plans to live a different and purposeful life, the "normies," the commoners, and the dumb take note. And like the Idiocracy they're rapidly becoming, they become jealous and start throwing hurdles in your way. They're too lazy, perhaps too stupid, to have a great life, and resent you pursuing greatness in yours. And by god if they can't have a great life, then nobody can.

Including you.

<u>Limiting Greatness</u>

When young and idealistic you will be…well…young and idealistic. You'll think you can achieve anything. You'll think you can live your dreams. You'll believe nothing will stand in your way, and if it does, pure determination and hope will win in the end because that's the way it always happened in all those movies you watched. Of course, those are the movies and this is the real world. And once the artificial support system known as "school" ends, you learn very quickly as an adult just what a load of idealistic hokum you were fed for all those years.

However, that doesn't mean you can't have realistic dreams. That doesn't mean you can't achieve greatness in a feasible and real world capacity. And so after living several years in the post-school real world, your brain will recalibrate what dreams are feasible or not, develop new ones, and put together the beginnings of a plan to pursue and achieve those new goals of feasible greatness. And though you may not become "the astronaut" you wanted to be when you were younger, you may achieve greatness by becoming a petroleum engineer, a surgeon, an accomplished saxophone player, or successful entrepreneur.

There's just one problem.

While the overly optimistic fluffy-bunnies-poppy-cock propaganda you were fed in school did not reflect the realities of the real world, it did at least do one thing right. It encouraged you to pursue your dreams. Sadly, the same cannot be said of the real world because once society gets a hint, a mere whiff that you might have dreams and goals, that you might dare to become great, that you might dare to be better than average, out of every crack, corner, and alley people will come out and work against you and your dreams. And the sad pathetic reason they do this is because they can't stand knowing there are people out there who are better than them.

These inferior scum hinder your life in two ways. Consciously and unconsciously.

The unconscious resistance society will put up against your pursuit of greatness is precisely that, unconscious. People do not actively try to stop you or sabotage your efforts to pursue your dreams, they are the clueless turkeys that are surrounding the eagle. This is perfectly exemplified in the state of Wyoming.

If you ever visit, live, or do work in Wyoming you will quickly realize the general population is slower, dumber, and just not as smart as the average population. My experiences there led me to develop the rule of "The Wyoming Three," where you have to ask people three times to get something done right once.

Want a black Russian?
Be prepared to first be served a light beer and a shot of whiskey before you're telling the bartender how to make a black Russian.

Need your fuel injectors cleaned?
Bank on the mechanic rotating the tires and changing the spark plugs before he finally listens to the words coming out of your mouth and realizes "oh, you needed the fuel injectors cleaned."

Need to order a Subway sandwich at the Subway in Casper right off of I-90?
You will have to tell the "sandwich artist" three times that you wanted the steak and cheese foot long sub, not the tuna sandwich he started making you, nor the teriyaki chicken sub he made after that.

At first I was infuriated with Wyomingites, taking their stupidity personally. It wasn't until I realized they were really that slow, really that dumb that they were effectively a separate species and couldn't help it. In other words, most Wyomingites weren't maliciously trying to slow me down, obstruct my day, and prevent me from pursuing my life goals. They were like deer unconsciously jumping out in front of my motorcycle with no intention of killing me.

Still, this didn't change the fact they WERE slowing me down, they WERE obstructing my day, and they WERE preventing me from pursuing my life goals. But whereas Wyoming is a special case, it is a microcosm of reality for abnormally intelligent people everywhere. The world is staffed and operated by "normal" or "dumb" people and thus the entire infrastructure, the entire world we need to work with to realize our goals operates at a ***MUCH SLOWER*** speed than we do.

You could be a great entrepreneur, but you are guaranteed to invariably hire some idiot that will stop the presses, monkey wrench the factory, or drive the train off the rails.

You could be a great musician, but will have to endure scores of inferior ones costing you gigs, lessening your music, and crippling your career.

You could have discovered a new compound that would make your company billions and score you a big promotion, but your boss doesn't understand it and yells at you saying "your job isn't to discover new compounds!"

And whereas this is just the normal consequence of living in an Idiocracy, it is so universal and so prevalent, that it is like slogging through an uphill swamp to make even a modicum of progress in reaching your goals and dreams. In short, you can go Mach 5, but the infrastructure of society you need to operate in has a maximum speed of 5MPH.

It may not be on purpose, but is infuriating nonetheless.

Then there are people who do consciously obstruct your efforts to excel in life. People who either through greed, envy, malice, or just plain jealousy see you either aiming for greatness or actually achieving it and simply cannot abide it.

We've discussed these people before.

The entire education industry isn't so much jealous as they are greedy. They have no problems forcing you to stay in school for 20 years when they give you 10 years' worth of education in exchange. The money is just too good. But realize just how big a hurdle "Big Education" threw in between you and achieving your life goals. They essentially stole 10 years of your life (and roughly $75,000 in tuition) all so they could enrich a bunch of talentless worthless people posing as "teachers" and "professors." Again, it's nothing personal, but their greed cost you 10 years, 12% of your life. 12% of your life that could have been spent realizing your goals.

There's family and friends.

Though presumably "the most important people in your life," far too many family members and friends don't view you as a loved one, whose best interests they have at heart. They view you instead as a competitor, or even property who belongs to the "family" in spite of your desires, dreams, and abilities. I've had two clients now where their welfare-collecting mothers forbade their sons from attending college because they'd leave home and that would mean less of a Section 8 housing allowance. We all know a boyfriend or girlfriend who belittled their significant other from chasing their dreams be it college, a job, or the military. And the black community is rife where any attempt at good grades or the desire for excellence is mocked as "acting white."

This is particularly painful in that these are presumably the people who love you most in life. Unfortunately, these people love themselves more than you, viewing you as nothing more than an asset to serve them, and jealous when the asset dares to aspire to become something better. They not only provide no moral support in your pursuit of greatness, but anchor you down like the proverbial "crabs in a bucket." Tragically, this sometimes forces abnormally intelligent people to pay the egregious price of leaving their family and "loved ones" so that they might simply have a life of their own.

And then there's your bosses.

Those experts at compliance, obedience, conformance, and pure averageness. Not only are they unlikely to lead you in an effective manner that would allow for you to excel in your career or reach your potential, if you dare make any attempts at excellence they will likely come crashing down on you, perhaps even fire you. So there you sit, operating at 3% your capacity, with no hope for advancement, and your brain rotting away, just to keep a roof over your head. Even if you play your cards right you will at minimum have to tolerate these sick, subhuman sadists for years until your great entrepreneurial ideas come to fruition and set you free.

The funny thing, however, is even though you may have endured the prison known as school, the betrayal and loss of your family, and a decade under an incompetent buffoon posing as your boss, you haven't even achieved greatness yet. This is merely the STRUGGLE to achieve greatness (heck, just to stay alive). But while you may think once you've achieved greatness all your problems are over, think again. Because there's a lot of parasites in this world who want a piece of your greatness. And that's when your problems really start.

Again, any HONEST analysis of various government budgets will show 70% of the taxes are merely giving money from the productive members of society to the non-productive ones. From the producers to the parasites. And because of progressive taxation, the most productive in our society pay the most, while the least productive get the most.

This is not to be political, nor to besmirch or belittle those who are parasites, but merely to be descriptive and to tell you the financial reality of where the majority of your efforts in life will go.

If you are successful and that success translates into financial success, you can expect, at minimum, around 50% of your income and wealth to be given to other people who did not work anywhere near as hard as you. This is an Idiocracy after all and it is the people who determine how much of your money you're allowed to keep, and how much of your money you will give to them.

But while you would think after forking over half your life's work to other people would make them happy, it's quite the opposite. Those on the receiving end of your forced charity are typically the least intelligent of society and don't really bother looking at the federal budget, let alone contemplate the economics or morality of wealth redistribution. And they certainly do not care about the personal hell you went through to achieve whatever greatness it is you achieved in life. All they see is that you have more than them and are completely unaware of the parasitic relation they have with you. So instead of humility, humbleness, kindness, thanks, and shame they emote rank jealousy, which often turns to full blown hate.

You are not a captain of industry who made it possible for everybody to have internet in their homes.

You are an evil capitalist fat cat "One Percenter" who didn't earn the $1.5 billion in net worth (after tax) you saved.

You are not a surgeon who saved thousands of lives after spending 10 years in med school.
You are a "privileged" individual that the world bent over backwards for to merely hand you your career on a silver platter.

And you aren't financially stable because you spent less than you made.
Your parents were rich or you somehow inherited your wealth.

Alas, they demand more and more of your money, more and more of your greatness, all while spitting in your face and blaming you for their mistakes.

So when you take this all in, both in terms of what society does unconsciously to impede your march towards greatness, as well as the conscious efforts society takes to prevent you from attaining it...not to mention the outright thankless confiscation of it...oh, and let's not forget with a cherry of jealousy-laden-hatred on top of it...you start to view your fellow man for the obstructions they are with an increasing amount of disdain, disrespect, and hatred.

Welcome to the world of misanthropy.

Misanthropy

Let us be very clear what society, consciously or not, does when it comes to abnormally intelligent people pursuing the most important thing in their lives.

Society does everything in its power to stop them.

Conscious or not.
Malicious or not.

Society, as it is currently structured, does everything in its might to make sure smart people do not reach their full potential.

The idiot at the gas station who pays for his cigarettes and lottery tickets with a check.
The welfare queen with five different children from five different fathers.

The professors and teachers who managed to teach you nothing in 20 years of schooling.
The bosses who demand you unnecessarily commute two hours a day.
The Oprah's and politicians of the world telling everybody their mistakes are your fault.
And the parasites taking half your wealth while hating you for it.

All of them are in between you and the most important thing in your life, achieving greatness.

People who prevent us from enjoying our lives, living our lives, and achieving our goals are at best what we call "obstacles" and at worst what we call "enemies." The problem is people who fall into those categories account for nearly all of humanity. And since they directly threaten what is most important to us, not to mention usually aren't pleasant people to deal with anyway, abnormally intelligent people are practically compelled to hate their fellow man, hate humanity, and ultimately become misanthropes.

At first this may sound bigoted and pre-judgmental (and it is), but as far as abnormally intelligent people are concerned the rest of society just destroyed or severely limited the most important thing in their lives. They took away the one thing that matters most to them and that is their ability to achieve greatness. It would be no different than if you stole or killed a mother's child. So when you take away the most important thing abnormally intelligent people have in life, "misanthropy" comes nowhere near to describing the fierce loathing some of them have for the rest of humanity.

Still, society's decision to obstruct abnormally intelligent people instead of champion them not only leads them to misanthropy, but also forces a choice on them. Specifically, is it worth spending your one precious finite life pursuing greatness? If it's going to be this hard, and whatever greatness you achieve will likely be confiscated, not to mention the hatred and envy you'll likely receive on top of it, would not a life of leisure and hedonism be preferable instead?

The answer of which lies in whether you believe there's an afterlife, which introduces the topic of nihilism.

Nihilism

If you are religious or believe in an afterlife, the here and now on this planet is ultimately pointless and moot. God or Vishnu or Allah or whoever is up there, keeping a score card, and if you do what those people said to do 3,000 years ago or 1,500 years ago you will make it to "heaven" where you will see all your deceased relatives, all your passed-away loved ones, your childhood dog "Snuffles," and live in eternal bliss forever.

But if you have a high IQ you likely won't believe in such poppycock, and so you might logically deduce that the afterlife will be much like the "before-life" where you don't remember anything because...

you weren't around to.

You didn't exist. And just like you didn't exist before you were born, you won't exist after you are dead, meaning the only thing that really matters is the here and now on this planet today.

Nihilism is a dark philosophy in that it makes you realize you may not only be mortal, but you won't be immortal in the afterlife. It forces the human mind to realize it is ULTIMATELY finite, it is going to end, and end permanently. But perhaps the scariest thing about nihilism is the loss of consciousness. "You" as you have known yourself for all these years, being the most important thing in your entire life, the only existence you've ever known, will end. All your experiences, observations, epiphanies, memories, fun, feelings, and joys will be forever lost, and worse they were all pointless. You won't see Grandpa Jimmy. You won't see "Snuffles the Dog." You'll be over. The end. Blackness, except you can't even say "blackness" because you'd have to be conscious to recognize and acknowledge the blackness.

But for all the truly dark and macabre tenets of nihilism, it does do one thing. It forcibly makes you ponder a very important premise by which to live the rest of your live by. Because if you believe there is an afterlife you will behave and make decisions one way, and if you don't believe there's an afterlife, you will behave and make decisions *in a drastically different way*.

If you operate from the premise there's an afterlife, you presumably assume the Earth, the universe, and humanity will go on forever. You are also probably more likely to have children which means you have a vested interest in at least the immediate future of humanity. This will prompt you to pursue greatness and leave a legacy, in spite of all the hurdles society throws in front of you, because your achievements will continue to help humanity into the infinite future. Yes, today's society may not deserve a cure for cancer, a drug that extends life by 100 years, or a newer, cheaper, cleaner form of fuel. But you altruistically believe in the long term progress and advancement of humanity, as well as the long term rewards your greatness will create in perpetuity.

Additionally, there is the aspect of the afterlife where (according to pretty much all religions) "we are looking down on the Earth." We are looking down on the people we left behind. This implies we still have a vested interest in humanity, post-death, which would further advocate doing the best you can while you're here and while you can.

But if you operate from the premise of nihilism, all the long term, infinite, and perpetual incentives associated with an afterlife vanish. The only thing that matters is your life here and now which forces you to be much more selfish and much more immediate. You combine this with the misanthropy you're likely to develop and you'll invariably have no interest or incentive of "achieving greatness" since it's not only not rewarding, but it would benefit people you hate (not to mention, you won't be around to witness any of the consequences anyway).

This then gives the "misanthropic, nihilist, genius" three options.

Hedonism – You just plain don't care about society and only live for yourself. None of it matters anyway because when the sun turns to a super red giant it will consume the Earth destroying any evidence we ever existed. So you drink, do drugs, have sex, ride motorcycles really fast, read books, avoid work, collect government checks, and live a life of minimalism, all structured around ensuring you spend the maximum amount of your time on this planet on you. Your theoretical potential and "greatness" isn't worth your time, besides society doesn't deserve it anyway. So light up a Lucky, pour yourself another Rumpleminze, and find that cute Jennifer Aniston girl you saw running around.

Achieving Greatness Anyway – You have such a great passion for your field, you couldn't care less if you're rewarded or not, or if society deserves it or not. Your hedonism is pursuing your greatness and the only person's opinion you care about is yours. Don't like people, aren't particularly fond of women, but love electricity? Become Tesla. Want to play with rockets and don't particularly care if it's used to bomb innocent civilians? Who cares? Become Wehrner von Braun. It doesn't matter if history remembers you fondly, or remembers you at all. Just as long as you get to exercise your intellect and achieve your own personal standard of greatness.

The Playboy Pursuit of Greatness – This is a combination of hedonism and pursing greatness, but largely on your terms and only if it's worth your time. You don't put forth your full effort, you don't aim to realize your full potential, but demonstrate and achieve excellence when it suits you, is beneficial, and takes minimal effort. This turns the pursuit of excellent from a costly and life-consuming profession into that of a flippant intellectual sport or hobby. This usually manifests itself in the form of literature or philosophy, very much like Voltaire's and Socrates' criticisms of society. It's neither toil-intensive nor revolutionary work, but it has the hallmarks of "intellectual greatness" including literary excellence and a heavy dose of misanthropy. In short, you know society is preventing you from achieving your best, so you don't pursue it. But you don't go down without a fight either. You demand your pound of flesh, ensuring your greatest accomplishment is mocking society, ridiculing it, reminding them how inferior they are, while forever giving them the bird as you're slowly lowered into your grave.

Regardless, whether you're a nihilist, a misanthrope, a hedonist, or one who believes in the afterlife, the truth is that no genius ever reaches their full potential. The reason why is that what we can see in our minds, what we "know" we can do, isn't possible because we rely on an imperfect world. Society is not as intelligent or driven as us. Our institutions of employment and education are corrupt and incompetent. And a truly meritocratic government will never exist. Alas, achieving greatness is very much like watching a stripper. Your brain drastically overestimates what you're going to achieve, while reality ensures you're going to come nowhere near it.

CHAPTER 8
SOLUTIONS

The purpose of this book was not just to highlight the drawbacks or "curses" in having a high IQ, but to also provide understanding, analysis, and ultimately solutions to these problems. And while some solutions were already discussed in previous chapters, it would help to draw some overall lessons and actionable items from the entirety of this book to not only help ourselves, but anybody we might know who is abnormally intelligent.

Test Your IQ ASAP

The single most important thing you can do to avoid the vast majority of problems associated with having a high IQ is to test it as soon as possible. Arguably the largest price abnormally intelligent people pay is the confusion and hell that comes from living life as a highly intelligent person, yet not knowing it. Be it thinking you're dumb because you keep falling asleep in class, the insanity that comes in having an intellectual inferior as a boss, or having no idea why people around you "just don't get it," millions of abnormally intelligent people live DECADES, even

THEIR ENTIRE LIVES not knowing the cause of it all is their abnormal intelligence.

Testing your IQ, however, won't solve all your problems, but it will correctly diagnose the cause as well as eliminate an inordinate amount of frustration and confusion in your life had you never known. You'll know why you can do a day's worth of work in two hours, while it takes everybody else eight. You'll know why you have no desire to attend a loud, obnoxious night club and rather read a book. And, perhaps most importantly, you'll know for a fact you're not insane, it's just the world around.

However, in addition to merely assessing your IQ, you also need to understand precisely what it means in terms of your ability. My charcutier gunsmithing friend remembered being tested at 136 as a kid. He said he knew he was smart, but didn't think he was anything special. Certainly not Harvard or MIT worthy and consequently SEVERELY underestimated himself.

He was in the top .8%. Again *not 8%*. The top *8/10ths of 1% of all of society.*

He absolutely was MIT, Harvard, or astronaut material, it's just that nobody told him.

Ensure this does not happen to you. Not only get your IQ tested, but calculate your percentile rank within the human population so you understand precisely just how much raw mental talent you have and guarantee you do not squander it.

Train, Mentor, and Coach Your Children

As a parent of a high IQ child you need to convey precisely what being abnormally intelligent means and mentor them so they make the most of it. This does not mean you become a Tiger Mom forcing your child to learn the violin at three, the piano at four, and master calculus by six, but get them to understand their potential, give them the incentives needed to reach their potential, and caution them against the hurdles they are guaranteed to run into along the way. Simply understanding (and not yelling at them) why they fall asleep in class will certainly do wonders for their sanity, but getting them to understand that they CAN make it into MIT, they CAN become a surgeon, and they CAN become anything they want ensures they will not waste their natural gifts.

Train and Re-Evaluate Yourself

A sad fact is that there are millions of people walking around right now who are geniuses, but don't know it because they simply do not conform to the averageness that society rewards. They think they're dumb, bad employees, bad students, even mentally ill. But if you permit yourself the self-respect to at least test your intelligence, and entertain the theory that you're not the dumb one, but nearly everybody else is, you will be able to truly assess your own intelligence and perhaps even open up a new chapter in life.

If you find out that you are indeed intelligent, you need to re-evaluate your entire life in the context of the problems and environments discussed in this book. Does you being abnormally intelligent explain the majority of problems you've ran into in school, career, relationships, etc.? Do things make more sense if you realize you're in the top 1% of society's intelligent? If so, not only may most of your problems be resolved, but you may also be underestimating yourself and should try applying yourself in different and more challenging things.

Are you stuck working at K-Mart because that's all your parents ever suggested you could achieve?

Why not go to school for chemical engineering?

Are you a bored housewife or househusband who stays at home and takes care of the kids? Perhaps you may want to consider learning to program or writing a book when there's some down time?

Maybe you're in the military and only consider yourself a "dumb private?" You could become the next Ulysses S. Grant.

Again, you can't let society tell you how intelligent you are and, thus, what you're capable of. You need to assess that for yourself and tell society what you're going to do.

Get Through School as Soon as Possible

The biggest waste of time for abnormally intelligent people will be their educations. From K-College the average high IQ person will quite literally spend two, slow, lethargic, painful, and expensive decades learning what they could master in one. The simple question is, *"Why not master it in one?"*

If you consider the veritable idiots they're graduating from college today, any abnormally intelligent 14 year old should have no problem getting a college degree before they can legally drive. And certainly any abnormally intelligent 16 year old should be able to get a STEM degree before they can buy a pack of smokes. Still, while your son or daughter may have the intellectual capacity to do so, that doesn't mean your state's laws will allow for it. Depending on the state you're in, you or your children may not be able to graduate from high school until a certain age. There are ways around this in terms of home schooling, getting your GED at 12, or perhaps going to school out of state, but you will have to consult your state's education laws to find out for sure. Still, even if you can shave off two years of K-12 education, that's two additional years of your life you get back from the education system gulag which can be spent achieving greatness and enjoying your life.

But regardless of how early you can graduate from high school, there is no reason to wait until you're 18 to start in on college. Most states allow high school aged children to take college courses and earn college credit. So instead of waiting till you're 18, out of the house, poor, impoverished, and working a full time job to make ends meet, you might as well take college classes as early as possible, lessening the number of classes and years you'll have to attend university outside of the home.

Naturally, those financially dependent on your child's presence in school will protest the above measures arguing that he or she won't be "socialized" correctly. That if they hang out with mature 21 year old college students instead of their bully-prone, misbehaving, nose-picking, armpit-farting, sophomoric 14 year old idiot peers they'll suffer some kind of psychological trauma.

"Why, you can't have your child learning Calculus in college for credit! You need to have them getting the crap kicked out of them in gym class or falling asleep in English!"

Of course, that's assuming you're going to listen to those who work in the lowest-IQ profession as to what's best for your infinitely-more intelligent child.

In short, ensure you or your children attain their education as quickly as possible. Abnormally intelligent people simply can't wait until they're 25, nearly 1/3rd dead, to start being taken seriously by the real world.

Prioritize People in Your Life

While already covered in Chapter 5, the value of your fellow man cannot be overemphasized. Remember, the artificial environment of school misleads you into thinking your social life will always be full of equally intelligent people who have adequate time and finances to hang out with you. It will slowly end once school ends. This leaves what few equally intelligent people remain in your life worth more than their weight in gold. Never take them for granted and always be on the hunt for excellent conversationalists.

Do What You Like, Not What Society Tells You

Even if you did know you were abnormally intelligent, that doesn't mean you're independent minded. The combination of peer pressure, marketing, and social consensus is more than enough of a force to convince that superior little brain of yours you need to do "normal things" with "normal people." And night clubs and bars are a perfect example.

When you're young and inundated with all those advertisements for booze, cigarettes, beer, and night clubs, all showcasing very attractive people, you believe you *just have to* go to a night club. You *just have to* go to a bar. That's where all the excitement is. That's where all the cool people hang out. And that's where life is truly fun and rewarding.

Until you actually attend one.

The truth is I would gladly trade in all of my nightclubbing, party going, bar hopping, and one night stands for a third of the time playing Dungeons and Dragons with all my high school nerd buddies. It was more rewarding, it was much more fun, and in the long run proved to be much rarer.

Be it night clubs, bars, Oscar parties, television, The World Bowl, The Super Cup, The Stanley Series, in the end none of them compare to

poker with the guys
a girls' night out
fishing with your dad
hiking with your buddies
smoking cigars with your grandpa

or whatever it is you personally want to do.

Do not ignore your instincts.

If your friends all want to go to a club and you're saying to yourself *"that seems very loud and very boring,"* don't go.

If your buddies want you to go to a strip club and pay $20 for a strip tease, but you're saying to yourself, *"why would I pay $20 not to have sex, but be sexually tortured,"* don't go.

And if your friends want to see "Herkee Jerkee and Her Slippy-Skip Scrunchy Monkeys" in concert, while you would rather stay at home and read a book, don't go.

Too much time is wasted doing what you think you should do or what you think society wants you to do. Your life is too short and your intellect too valuable to be wasted on things that simply don't inspire you and are, frankly, beneath you.

Confidence Against Your Bosses

While you may need your boss more than he or she needs you, and while you would like to have food on the table and a roof over your head, the amount of mental anguish and abuse you'll suffer at the hands of psychotic, sadistic, controlling bosses is not worth it. If I were to do it all over again, I would have bought a van and lived in it rather than tolerate the years under the amoral, inferior scum that constituted the majority of my bosses.

However, you do not have to live in a van or stay at home until you're 30 in the anticipation of getting fired as you tell your bosses off. You just simply have to let go of any moral qualms you have about collecting a government check and going on welfare.

The truth is we live in a democracy and, for better or worse, we have voted in an elaborate system of government social programs that will pretty much take care of your every need. You won't be rich, you may not even be able to afford a car, but it is better eating government cheese and living in Section 8 housing than going into work, day in, day out to deal with a sadist and psychopath as a boss. You do yourself no favors "taking the high road," refusing government handouts, while you sustain increasing levels of psychological damage and trauma.

Tell your boss to FOAD.
Make them fire you.
Collect unemployment, welfare, EBT, and Medicaid if you have to.
And live off of them for a change.

Because it just isn't worth the mental price you pay.

Furthermore, in being willing to collect a government check not only will you refuse to tolerate one iota of abuse from your bosses, but you will also be able to play hardball with them, which ironically sometimes results in better success than trying to make them happy. Many bosses, understand, are used to bossing their underlings around and NEVER having anybody stand up to them. And most of them, since they are bullies, only respond to threats, violence, or bullying back. In hindsight the handful of times I went into my bosses' offices and read them the riot act, threatened to report them to the feds, or simply stood up for myself I was never fired. They actually stood down. So if you have nothing left to lose and are willing to go on the government dole, your mental health is absolutely worth playing hardball with your boss, even bluffing for a better position or better treatment.

Entrepreneurship ASAP

As mentioned before, entrepreneurship and self-employment is likely the only form of employment abnormally intelligent people can endure. However, unless you have rich parents or are to inherit a company previously founded by a family member, you will have to at least spend some time working for someone else. Unless you are very fortunate, this job is practically guaranteed to be beneath you and will not provide your mind with the mental and professional stimulation it needs. So it's just best to plot your escape to self-employment as soon as possible.

How soon?

Ideally, even before you enter the work force.

A client of mine was working at a fast food restaurant in Australia. He was making $8 per hour, but his boss was also embezzling tips from the employees. After telling him to go to the authorities, I found out he and his father were running an informal computer repair shop in their basement. I asked him what they charged and he said around $25 per hour.

I said, *"Dude, what are you doing working at the fast food joint??? Go set up a web site and start offering your computer repair services to the public! If you play your cards right and get various computer and IT certifications you may never have to go to college and never have to work for anybody EVER!"*

He has since quit his fast food job and is now pursuing his foray into self-employment at the age of 16.

The point is the sooner you start down the path of entrepreneurship, the sooner you will be free of the bonds of traditional employers and the more time you'll have in your life to enjoy it. So whether you're a high school kid, a college student, or a 32 year old corporate cubicle slave, start now.

And don't just start now, start while you're on the job.

Bored in English class? Start working on your business ideas.
Bored in college? Start researching the industry you're interested in with the college's wifi.
Finished all your work by 10AM because you're that smart? Start teaching yourself accounting (which is a skill ALL entrepreneurs need).

The sooner you discover that successful business idea the sooner you can leave corporate America forever, not only setting yourself free, but rewarding your mind with a truly rewarding career.

Sublimation, Booze, and Drugs

Tempted, even called for, as you may be to use booze and drugs for a temporary escape from the real world, it's a slippery slope that can lead to addiction. And while many abnormally intelligent people would never regret their use (even abuse) of alcohol and controlled substances, there are healthier options, namely staying active and sublimation.

If you have a choice of the "three drugs" discussed in Chapter 6 channeling your excess mental energies towards productive and beneficial activities is better for you in the long run than drug or alcohol addiction. There is certainly the risk (more likely, the guarantee) you'll build up a tolerance to novelty, and let's not kid ourselves, booze and drugs are just much more effective (not to mention fun) when it comes to numbing your brain to the various mental challenges in life, but staying active and pursuing new hobbies is better for you in the long run than merely chemically checking yourself out from society for a couple hours every day.

This isn't to say you shouldn't enjoy the occasional cocktail, or even get completely blotto from time to time, but boozing and drugs do not provide agency or purpose in life. Merely wonderful, blissful avoidance.

Unsolvable

Finally, as are with many things in life, there may simply be no solution to your problems. Not all problems are solvable. Not all problems have answers. They are cold, hard, unfortunate, and unchangeable facts in life that you must accept and deal with. But the real threat "unsolvable problems" present is not the constant and never-ending pain they force you to endure during your entire life. It's when you try to solve them that they are infinitely more damaging. Because as painful as it is to tolerate these unsolvable problems in life, it is much more painful trying to solve them, as that is the fastest and most guaranteed path to insanity.

The End

ADDITIONAL BOOKS AND RESOURCES BY AARON

Books

"Worthless"
"Bachelor Pad Economics"
"Enjoy the Decline"
"The Black Man's Guide Out of Poverty"
"Captain Capitalism – Reserved"

Internet

Consultancy
http://www.assholeconsulting.com

The Clarey Podcast
https://soundcloud.com/aaron-clarey/

Blog
http://captaincapitalism.blogspot.com

YouTube
https://www.youtube.com/user/AaronClarey

Twitter
https://twitter.com/aaron_clarey

Printed in Great
Britain
by Amazon